A HILLWALKER'S JOURNAL

CALAMITIES

ISBN:

First paperback edition 2022

CONTENTS

PROLOGUE

The baking sun had disappeared some time ago when we were down in the foothills; wearing shorts, T-shirts and sunglasses. Once we reached higher ground the sky became a milky haze of thin cloud and the sun's radiance was reduced to a faint glow. Now it was getting colder near the top; we were surrounded by darker clouds, which drifted menacingly before our eyes. As the ground levelled out, it seemed that the climbing had finished and we stood there, panting heavily, legs aching. Chris stopped, sat down and I followed suit.

What next? and where are we? I would have said - but I was still trying to catch my breath. Then the clouds opened up in front of us, like curtains revealing the next act. I could see a jagged ridge leading up to the peak of Helvellyn. The ridge had a sheer drop on either side that plunged into unimaginable depths that seemed both surreal and captivating. Various people were scuttling their way across the ridge, clinging to the rock like ants: these people were clinically insane.

"That's it - Striding Edge," said Chris catching his breath after two hours of hill climbing.

"Jesus Christ! this is madness. Do we …. have to go across that?" I said, needlessly pointing to the ridge. Is it safe?"

Chris just smiled, enjoying my baptism of fire - perhaps a little too much. My introduction to hill walking involved going across "Striding Edge" and he had really pulled a fast one - and he knew it.

"Think of the next part as not a 'ridge' but a 'bridge to Helvellyn'."

"A bridge to hell – that's a great thought," I laughed.

I stood and stared at a dramatic knife edge ridge that could have surely only existed in a Tolkien novel; but now I could see in front of me - a crazy paving ridge with giant drops on each side. My legs began to quiver as I tried to imagine myself following those other scramblers into a suicide mission. There are many descriptions I could allude to, but walking a tightrope two thousand feet above the ground reflects my first reaction. I could not fully comprehend the scale of this ridge and the gaping drops on each side. I had never seen anything like this before and the view in front of me was truly awesome and petrifying in equal measures.

Chris had sensed my reluctance to go further, and he was already walking forwards.

"We can't go back now, we came all this way. It's not as narrow as it looks, the ridge is really quite wide…in places," said Chris moving down to the start of the ridge. "Just follow me."

I looked behind me. It would have been humiliating to turn around. I tentatively followed Chris, as if my life depended on it - and right now that seemed to be the case.

As we began to traverse the ridge I crouched low, like an old drunken spider. My plan for surviving the ridge was based on staying low and clinging to the rocks with three or four points of contact. Standing up was not really an option for me as my legs were like jelly, so I considered that the crawling method was better for sticking close to the rocks; I was only twenty-five and I had my whole life ahead of me. I looked at Chris who was walking upright, as if going for a morning stroll hands in pockets; he was taking confident strides along the upper path which seemed safer.

"You're a mad bastard," I muttered to myself as Chris looked behind him to see me trailing behind.

"You'll get used to it," said Chris as he wiped the sweat from his forehead, and blinked fiercely as the sun made a brief entrance through the clouds.

Occasionally, I peered over the ridge to the right, which revealed a sheer drop into a tarn, very far below, God knows how far down, and to my left – an even steeper vertical drop into some kind of abyss. I quickly decided that looking down was not helping my wobbly legs and I tried (albeit with some difficulty) to pretend that these drops did not exist. I continued across the arête moving like a sick crab but getting into some kind of routine. Then, I had to climb down a bloody awkward rock, which was known as "a bad step" (another classic understatement found in walking books) and Chris had to verbally coach my feet onto something that seemed solid. Then he scuttled down to a lower section and with a small amount of joy, like a toddler finding a lost toy, he pointed out a gravestone erected in honour of somebody who had fallen off Striding Edge. This was really not very helpful: my nerves were already in tatters. At the end of the ridge, we scrambled up a steep scree slope to the summit of Helvellyn and the clouds had drifted away to reveal a panoramic view of the lake district peaks. Chris pointed out other mysterious peaks like Skiddaw, Scafell and Great Gable. I threw my rucksack on the floor and we sat down next to the trig point and I drank heavily from my water bottle.

"Did you enjoy Striding Edge?" said Chris as he tucked into his ham and Djon mustard sandwich.

"Yeah, it was good," I said unwrapping the cling film from my cheese and piccalilli sandwich which had been squashed flat by my ridiculously heavy flask.

I stood up whilst chewing, and felt the sudden coolness of the breeze ripple through my sweaty t-shirt that had been clinging to my back. I keep looking around at the views: green and brown mountain peaks everywhere, blue lakes in the valleys below. I was glowing with pride, standing on a mountain peak over 1,000 metres high (or 3,000 ft in old money); but I couldn't take my eyes away from Striding Edge. That was 1993: and I knew that I was already hooked on hill walking.

During the next couple of years I enthusiastically participated in several walks: Coniston Old Man, the Sandstone Trail (Cheshire), the Gritstone Trail (Derbyshire) and Offa's Dyke (Welsh borders) – which all involved one or two days camping, with Chris and Ric. These trips were a combination of fun and hell in equal doses; but thankfully the painful memories were erased by the brain and somehow after a month or two everybody had forgotten the hell, and were raring to go again on the next "walk". The painful memories of foot blisters, aching limbs and the sore shoulders resulting from carrying excessive weight, could be turned into funny stories. It had always seemed like a good idea to carry camping gear over long distances in those days: the enthusiasm of youth takes precedence over pragmatism. The brain only remembers the lofty peaks, the spectacular views and the morning sun; nostalgia is a close companion to the deluded.

Then in January 1995, Howard and I embarked upon our first epic adventure into the winter wonderland of the Lakes. Our target was Skiddaw – it was our first ascent. The usual walking tracks were hidden, and that was my excuse for going up the mountain the wrong way. The weather was perfect that day; bright sunshine, clear blue skies and the ground was covered by a white carpet of deep snow. We went up via the south side of Skiddaw (by accident) and had to make our trail in the virgin snow. Although we didn't know how to climb a mountain in the deep snow, we just improvised and managed to kick in our own steps most of the way up to the summit. We had the mountain to ourselves. At the top we could see the nearby

magnificent Blencathra to the east and to the west the Scafells painted white – almost

unrecognisable. The low winter sun created a dazzling white effect, and we were soon joined

on the broad summit by four bearded middle aged walkers, who looked like they knew what

they were doing. I noticed that they had proper winter gear, huge boots and trekking sticks.

Not long after they walked past us on the broad summit ridge, one of middle aged men was

shouting something and pointed up to the sky,

"Look Tom – look! I can't believe it!" one of the men shouted in a broad Yorkshire accent.

The others looked up to the sky and together they made a roaring noise "Wooooaaahhhh!".

Suddenly, the second man dropped to his knees as if he had seen the second coming.

Howard and I paced over to the men to join in the madness. One of them pointed at a circular

light beam in the sky.

"It's a Broken Spectre!"

"We've been walking hills for thirty years and we have never seen this in our lives…. it is a

moment to be treasured," said the man nearest to me.

Howard and myself gazed at the circular rainbow, with some curiosity, and tried to capture it

on camera (God loves a trier).

As all three men had now dropped to their knees and started wailing as if performing a pagan

ritual, things started to get even more strange. One of the men, possibly the one with the

biggest beard, stood up and stretched out his arms and legs to form a human "X" shape. It

was at this point that his X shadow appeared in the centre of the circular light in the sky. It created a very strange symbol (like the TV programme *World in Action* logo show in the credits).

I looked at my water bottle and then at Howard.

"Oh my God. A yellow shaped circle in the sky. This is getting weird," said Howard smiling and screwing his face up in disbelief.

"These guys have gone crazy, maybe this a really big deal. I have never heard of this "Broken Spectre" thing, It's very strange," I said in earshot of the Yorkshiremen.

When things had calmed down the four men began to act normal and they began chatting to us. They had climbed mountains across the world and had just returned from a mountain expedition in Georgia, but they had never seen a Broken Spectre…until now.

Even though Howard and I were ignorant novices, we had still felt privileged to witness the Lake District at its best and on such a beautiful day. The Broken spectre was the icing on the cake; apparently it was a once in a life-time experience.

"If you don't have crampons, you'll be needing some sticks to get down from this mountain. it's very slippery on those paths," said one of the men with sunglasses, and red skin that was the same colour as his red beard.

"Yeah sure," I said feeling that I was being patronised by this old mountain warrior. Sticks were accessories like handbags: going down on the main route was going to be a doddle, surely. Howard was also wondering what all the fuss was about.

"Sticks?" said Howard.

We soon found out what the fuss was all about as we walked downhill, on the main route (north side) from Skiddaw on the icy paths and we both slipped over countless times. The first few times it was funny. It became less funny after slipping over a dozen times – each time crashing our knees or butts onto the icy rocks. We finally reached the bottom, if you know what I mean –battered and bruised, vowing to buy walking sticks.

******

Ten years after Striding Edge I decided to start a journal, to record my experiences of mountain walks in the UK, Europe, Middle East and Africa between 2007 and 2016. Each walk had its own story, and its own adventure. Each walk had different characters and changeable weather conditions. This journal tells the stories from my perspective – hopefully they are faithful to the facts; well, the jury is still out on that one. Here's the thing: all walkers have a different views on risk, weather impacts, equipment, navigation and the human condition. Perhaps this is why "walking" "hiking" "climbing" (whatever you want to call it) is associated with memorable adventures – except that my memory is selective.

I hope you enjoy reading these journals. Just in case you think you have wasted your money on this book, I can confirm that fifty per cent of profits will be directed to a Cumbrian mountain rescue charity and the other fifty per cent will go towards a new pair of walking boots. If you see me hopping around with only one boot – then the book sales have not gone too well.

MY FELLOW WALKERS

I was very fortunate that most of my friends were keen hillwalkers – so, there were always people ready to accompany me on the hiking trips that we planned on certain weekends. In the interest of integrity and confidentiality I have listed the real names of my friends below: what do you expect? this is a serious piece of non-fiction; and besides, everybody knows that a married man with three kids is not worth suing.

In alphabetical order.

ANDY MCKAY, well known for ice climbing, flying gliders, paragliding, and any activity that involved being "high up" and dangerous. Andy and Aran had camped up at 3,800 metres near the Aguille de Midi Telegraphic and stayed there for two weeks; for reasons unknown.

Andy wasn't keen on hillwalking and he had a successful track record of avoiding most of our walking trips. To be fair, Andy did enjoy winter climbs and I do recall Andy guiding us on a roped up winter climb across Sharp Edge.

ARAN BYRNE, a regular hillwalker, a dedicated follower of outdoor clothing fashion, and loved to get high. On every walk, Aran modelled new items of clothing that acted as a catalyst for discussions and an healthy amount of envy. Aran usually carried a vast array of food and equipment to cover every type of scenario. If anybody finds a large tin of rice pudding at the foot of the Eiger - its Aran's.

CHRIS PUDDEPHATT, was a regular walker with hillwalking in his blood. Chris always had the determination to get high and make it to the top- on every walk. He introduced me to walking in the hills and I am eternally grateful for this.

GARY SMITH (the author)was a regular walker who liked to get high and stay high. He was at his happiest on the high ridge routes that had been plotted from the comfort of his armchair. He was a reluctant follower of outdoor clothing fashion and stoically resisted new-fangled walking equipment such as solar panel battery chargers and walking poles. He possessed a sufficient amount of blind optimism to tackle challenging peaks but his success was compromised by a fear of heights and a stubborn refusal to "turn back" whilst under the wicked spell of summit fever.

GEOFF PATCH, was a regular walker who had been higher than any other walker that I know. Geoff had that rare combination of having all the gear *and* the ideas. He was super organised, fit and understood the dark art of navigation. He could smell the mountain and calculate the risk. Despite the above deficiencies I was surprised that Geoff's plans to get high actually resulted in such a prolific record of peak bagging. My main worry about Geoff was that he wore the same light blue shirt on every single walk, which he assured me was washed regularly – the Jury is out on that one.

HOWARD BLYTHE, was a regular walker who enjoyed getting high in the mountains. Howard was always sure footed and smiled his way cheerfully through the predictable and unpredictable chaos that unravelled on a number of walks.

JERRY SYKES, was the oldest person in our group of walkers, but he was very fit and had a good tolerance for hardship; he rarely complained – which was nice because there was usually quite a lot to complain about. Jerry had a careless quality in the way he dressed, ignoring outdoor clothing fashions with a blunt panache. Jerry's approach to outdoor clothing and walking equipment was old and minimalistic which was the complete opposite to Aran's. Jerry had the unfortunate tendency to fall over at critical moments; such as river crossings or snow slopes. Jerry possessed bucket loads of cheerfulness, and a sufficient amount of blind optimism to join each walking party. Despite Jerry's senior years he possessed a spectacular surplus of head hair. His shoulder length hair was of a greater quantity than all of the walker's combined above.

LESLEY MCKAY, was and still is a keen hillwalker. She loves the Lake District; but we never saw her get high because of poor visibility. For reasons unknown, she only joined our walking party once (see "The Scafell Return") and never again. Lesley and Andy are married so I guess they must have compared notes on the pros and cons of joining our walking trips, and made their decisions accordingly.

GRAN PARADISO - 30ᵀᴴ MAY 2007

"Men dull in mind find no cause for wonder anywhere; they idly sit at home instead of going to see what is on view in the great theatre of the world." Gesner 1541.

The Gran Paradiso is located in the Gran Paradiso National Park in northwest Italy, and it is the highest mountain, 13,323 ft (4,061 metre), entirely within Italy and the culminating point of the Graian Alps. In September 1860 the Englishman John Cowell became the first to reach the summit of the mountain. In 2007, six other Englishmen - who had never heard of this mountain before, climbed it.

Our party of six men (all in various stages of mid-life crisis) had been planning to climb Mont Blanc in 2007. From the safety of the armchair, basic research suggested that climbing Mont Blanc was achievable for reasonably fit and experienced hikers. Howard, Chris, and myself were experienced hillwalkers who had plodded around the Lake District and Snowdonia for several years. We had ventured on occasional scrambles on the likes of Sharp Edge, Striding Edge and Crib Goch, and that was the closest we got to mountaineering. We had built up some confidence and we were ready to go the Alps and have a crack at Mont Blanc. Aran and Andy were also old school pals but they had done some rock climbing in the Alps and the UK before, so they knew how to use all those mysterious pieces of climbing equipment such as ropes, clips, harnesses and most impressively of all…rope knots. Twenty years ago, Aran and Andy had camped out high up near the Mont Blanc massif via the telegraphic (the Aguille de Midi) station, for several weeks to acclimatise at 4,000 metres.

The acclimatisation was a very British affair, which involved drinking lots of tea and making plans without actually doing much. Aran and Andy had risked their lives each morning when they left their tent to traverse a knife edge ridge to enter the Aguille de Midi telegraphic station to buy that cup of tea, and walk back along the same ridge again: it must have been a good cup of tea. Although they were camping for four weeks their summit attempt via the Gouter route was cancelled as they were battered back by strong winds. For Aran and Andy, they wanted to try again, and reach the summit. Twenty years later, they were back in Chamonix, this time drinking coffee, and making plans.

For hillwalkers like Howard, Chris and myself, we had not used ropes before, and somehow ropes equalled danger. Rope knots to novices are a real puzzle, like black magic; but to rock climbers they are second nature.

Aran brought along a friend and work colleague from London, called Jerry who looked a bit like Peter Stringfellow. We had met Jerry on a couple of walks and he seemed very polite, easy going and above all seemed ready to embrace the potential for unexpected chaos as much as the rest of us. Quite simply we all had one thing in common; the spirit of adventure. But let's be honest here, we were hoping for glory; bagging the biggest and most famous peak in Western Europe. There is a fine line between optimism and delusion. The other option is pessimism, and the difference is that the latter stays in the house glued to the sofa.

The only additional gear we needed was crampons, an ice axe and …sunglasses to protect ourselves from the dazzling reflection from the sun against the white snow. Sometimes the planning of these expeditions and the anticipation of what might happen is more exciting than the event itself. There were restless nights thinking about the dangers which included altitude sickness, rockfall, avalanches, and slipping off the Gouter ridge. These dangers are somehow counteracted by the achievement of reaching the peak of Mont Blanc and getting back down again to tell stories about the adventure.

For some reason, and I'm not really sure why, we decided to plan our trip to Mont Blanc in May. This is a period of time when the snow depths are traditionally high, and the weather is not the most favourable. Chamonix locals recommend September as the best time as the snow is generally in better condition and the peak tourist times in July and August have passed.

Aran (who is fluent in French) had arranged for a French guide to take the six of us up to Mont Blanc. When we reached Chamonix, we met up with Patrick in a bar, and as we sipped our cold beers the depressing news was slowly released that the weather conditions for Mont Blanc were 'not good' at this time. After all of the hype and expectation, Mont Blanc would have to wait for another year (or perhaps forever). Due to out-of-season Gouter hut closure and heavy snow on all other routes our guide proposed the Gran Paradiso mountain as an alternative.

The Gran Paradiso was a 4000m peak that we had previously never heard of, but it was still a "4,000 metre alpine peak" and what else were we going to do?

The six of were sharing a tent at a campsite, near the river in Chamonix. We were quite pleased when we booked the campsite because we were keeping the cost of our eight days in Chamonix down to a minimum. The campsite was cheap: it consisted of a toilet/shower block, a small shop and a field. Also with a cheap *easyJet* flight from Liverpool, plus the hire car costs between six of us, we could be proud of ourselves from the budgeting perspective. One million students would have been proud of us.

In reality it was slightly different, as we weren't teenagers anymore and quickly found that it was very difficult to sleep in a tent with six snoring middle aged men. It was hot during the day and cold at night, so during the day when we were waiting for the clouds to lift themselves out of the valley we sought refuge in McDonalds. Anything was better than to go back to the wet, smelly campsite. In terms of diet and rest – it a wasn't a healthy or relaxing preparation for an Alpine expedition.

On 30th May 2007 , we woke up to find the orange roof of our tent had turned white and was much lower than usual.

"Hey, lads, it's been snowing overnight," said Chris as he lay on his belly with his head stuck out of the tent.

"Wow. There's loads of snow. Can you imagine what it's like that on the peak of the Gran Paradiso?" said Aran.

We all groaned in response. Maybe there would be no mountain to climb if there was avalanche risk.

"Well, today we're going to climb that mountain in Italy, what's it called, the Grand…" I said.

"…Gran Paradiso," said Andy with a weariness of somebody having to repeat himself too many times.

"That's the one," I said.

We were surprised how heavily it had been snowing overnight, as there were six inches of snow covering the grass, and pretty much everything else. The morning sun beamed down to the bottom of the valley, and we started to leave the tent one by one and tramp over to the toilet/shower block. Breakfast consisted of half-eaten cold snacks that we found in our rucksacks, and then we packed the cars up: the mood amongst our group was good. This was because we were actually going away from the camp site to climb a mountain. We had spent several days of sitting round the campsite, wandering around Chamonix, checking weather reports on the internet and then re-checking at the Chamonix weather centre just to confirm the same depressing news that conditions on the peaks were too cloudy, snowy or windy. We set off towards the Italian alps. As we cruised along the sun drenched valley roads we bounced along to the sounds of Kasabian blasting from the Skoda stereo: life didn't get much cooler than this. As we passed underneath the Mont Blanc Tunnel, we realised that this might the closest we would ever get to Mont Blanc. We met up with our two guides, Patrick and Mouro at the car park at Pont (1960 metre). The guides were in deep conversation as they stood in the deep snow of the car park. They were speaking in French about the weather report and Mouro was pointing at the snow and did not seem very keen on the task ahead of us. Patrick scooped up a lump of snow from the car park, and they scanned the foothills as Mouro pointed upwards at the peaks, shaking his head slowly with a sad expression as if his puppy had been taken away from him.

The six of us stood in a group doing our own risk assessment.

"Well, we've come all this way, we may as well have a go at the Gran Paradiso," said Aran as he extended one of his walking poles.

"Shit, they're going to cancel the trip," I said.

"Aran, what are they saying?" said Andy

"I don't exactly know, they've started speaking in Italian now…it seems they are not happy about the depth of the snow," said Aran.

After the two guides had finished their discussion in various languages, they beckoned us forwards and started walking on the path that crossed the small river and we followed - buzzing with excitement. It was a kind gesture by the Italians to build this bridge to prevent Jerry from falling into the river: Jerry had a rather chequered history of river crossings; which will be explained later on in this journal . We began to ascend on a zig zagged path through the forest and up the snowy mountain to finally reach the Victor Emmanuel II mountain hut around 4.30 p.m. This mountain hut was so good, it would be rude not write a few words about Victor.

Vittorio Emanuele II was the first king of the united Italy. He was also a very keen hunter who used the area as his private hunting domain. After his death in 1878, he was succeeded by his son Umberto I who was assassinated in 1900, and replaced by his grandson Victor Emmanuel III. Although Victor resigned from office in 1946 when Italy became a republic, it was Victor Emmanuel III, not much into hunting, who handed the area over to the Italian state in 1922; hence it became Italy's first national park.

The first day's walking had been straightforward, and the deep snow had not been a problem, so far. We sat outside the hut resting our feet, reflecting that the four hour trek was similar to a 3,000 feet Lake District peak in wintertime. At this point we were now at 2,710 Metres (9485 ft in old money). I was surprised that even at this level the higher altitude was noticeable on the lungs. After days of rain and mist of Chamonix it was nice to bask in the sun and dry out our kit in the new surroundings of the impressive Italian Alps. We made the most of it, enjoyed a beer and mingled with some jovial Dutch students in a perfect Alpine setting of sun, forest and snow-capped mountains.

The food in the hut was cheap, simple and supplied in ample quantities (unlike Chamonix on all three accounts!). Unfortunately there was not much sleep for me being in a room near the only toilet; just to be clear, that is one toilet shared between 150 people. The upside of this unfortunate location was that I began to suffer from diarrhoea .....no further details required.

Breakfast consisted of a stale slice of bread with Jam and some coffee - which hardly seemed worth delaying the starting time for. We set off at 6.00a.m. for the long hike to the summit.

The hut to the summit route involves a height gain of 1350m, often completed on average four to five hours, but after the moraines section we waded through continuous snow between one and three feet deep, all the way up. We realized that this was going to be a long slog and the guides were anxious to press on.

At 6.30 a.m. the sun was shining on the mountains in the west as if a light switch had been clicked and now there were so many mountains on view: it was a privilege to be here.

The deep snow was hard work and was it hampering our progress. In some cases we had to make our own tracks. Constantly taking big steps was becomes tiring and the air became thinner, and suddenly the general chit chat stopped and people conserved their energy.

As we climbed higher Andy pointed out some spectacular views of Mont Blanc and the Matterhorn. It was at this early stage that I noticed my water bladder drinking tube had frozen up, so that from now on I had no access to my water. My only option was to beg the others for water… this was not a good situation. I became worried about dehydration.

Near the top of a particularly steep slope, the surface changed from walkable snow (where it was possible to kick in steps) to thin powder covering ice that could hardly be dented with the toe of the boot. We tried in vain to kick in footholds: It was simply not suitable for boots and we leant heavily on our sticks for support. In hindsight, we realized that we should have put our crampons on at the bottom of this slope, because now it was too steep to fiddle around with crampons. "Axes!" shouted Aran. "Your sticks are fucking useless here lads!" All eight of us were bunched up in a traffic jam on the ice slope where further progress required an axe. It was an oversight, because our axes were packed away in our rucksacks – so we didn't have these to hand.

Just then, almost on cue Howard slipped over.

"Aaahhhh!" shouted Howard as he slipped head-first, landing flat on his stomach, and began to slide down the mountain. I looked around and could not reach Howard from where I was standing, and to be honest I was having enough trouble keeping my own balance.

Luckily, Mouro was close enough, and he grabbed him before his slide gathered momentum – saving him from a potentially nasty accident. Everybody quickly rummaged into their rucksacks and swapped their sticks for axes: this was not an easy manoeuvre whilst balancing on a steep slope with your toes for grip – it was a short, sharp introduction to winter walking.

Once over the slope we were greeted by an icy north easterly wind: we all had a brief ten minute stop to put our crampons on. The cold had a biting effect on my wet, gloveless hand whilst tying the crampons on, and it wasn't an easy task because there are so many straps to get right. At this point one of Jerry's gloves blew off down the slope in an accelerating spinning motion like a leaf in the autumn wind. It disappeared over the lip of the slope. Jerry made a belated move to chase it, but within a few seconds the glove had vanished down the slippery slope.

"Leave it, it's not worth it!" I shouted. Luckily, Jerry used his spare gloves anyway. Then we were all roped up (two groups of four, with a guide leading each) at this point we were advised about the presence of crevasses. *Crevasses?* Nobody had mentioned crevasses on the Gran Paradiso. Crevasses were cracks in the glacier that could range from 1 metre deep to an endless drop into an abyss; some people who fell into these bottomless pits were never seen again. Sometimes this could become a sociable disaster as there is a possibility of dragging your (roped up) mates down the same crevasse one by one– if they did not become a human anchor to stop the slide. Our leader of four was Mouro an Italian guide who spoke very little English and "helpfulness" wasn't really included in the deal. The other half of our group was in a separate party on front with the popular (and English speaking) French guide Patrick, who had taken us out on the Mer De Glace a few days earlier for some crampons and ice practice.

The pace of our rope party (Mouro, Howard, me and Jerry) seemed to be in short bursts, and with no set rhythm; slowly we edged up the snow slopes of the summit like a caterpillar. Despite the fact that we were all roped up together, we wanted to go at our individual paces – it was a difficult marriage to say the least. Mouro was irritating me as he seemed to be on mission to race to the top and get back home for teatime. He wasn't going to achieve any records with me in tow - I was struggling to keep pace. I was also carrying a heavy load of excuses: diarrhoea in the night, no water left to drink, my body was beginning to suffer in the altitude. I'd never felt like this before on British peaks, but the others seemed to be in better shape; I was falling apart. I noticed that that my heart was beating incredibly fast and then I started to feel slightly lightheaded and slurring my speech.

I was trying to work out if I had consumed the target two litres of liquid for the climb. I had drunk possibly ¾ litre before the water bladder had frozen, and had eaten three energy sachets. This was to be my total consumption for the day, apart from some swigs from Howard's water bottle: every drop was precious.

Each time we conquered a slope another huge slope appeared before our eyes, and we could see our other friends in front snaking their way up the mountain ahead of us. The timing of stops became a frustration for Mouro who looked like he had been slapped by a wet fish every time one of our party requested a water break. Photo stops were now out of the question.

Italian-English relations were not helped by our respective lack of language skills. Speaking became limited to shouts of "stop!" and then for slow pace we shouted "piano".

For at least the next few hours we continued the ascent, heads down, concentrating on the deep steps already imprinted in the snow. The rhythm became a trance-like trudge 'one foot in front of the other', except my breathing was irregular and my pulse beat was racing so it was difficult to take my mind off the task in hand. At this point (as with many long walks) where silence becomes the norm and people tend to go within themselves, collect their own thoughts, ask questions such as; why the hell am I doing this ? is it the physical challenge? the spiritual fulfilment of being at one with nature? or a week away from the monotonous nine-till-five? The answer is probably all of the above to varying degrees.

Others were finding the walking through deep snow for long periods an impossible task. Some guys from Buxton (England) who had set off from the hut before us using snowshoes, had slowed down and were now really struggling. We saw them turn round. The possibility dawned on me that this so-called easy 4,000 metre climb would not be achievable. Amazingly the Dutch party (eight university students) although they were roped up had no crampons or axes, and they were relying on walking sticks alone on the upper slopes.

For the last few hundred metres near the summit and I was requesting a rest every ten paces. It became difficult to get an audible request out of the tightening lungs. I had clearly exceeded my quota of "piano!" and "rest!" shouts and Howard was bitterly complaining about this as he (not surprisingly) wanted to press on quickly get this summit climb out of the way. Jerry followed doggedly at the rear and was generally very "British" and stoical about the whole ascent. He didn't complain one bit, and I'm not sure I would have been as diplomatic as Jerry.

It was at this point that Mouro had discovered his tongue and he turned round and said "Gareee, why you not singing today?". I could have told him fuck-off, as he was smiling at me, enjoying my misery but my mouth was as dry as a parrots cage and I didn't have the energy to speak, never mind swear. Now don't get me wrong, Mouro's mother probably loves him and he is probably kind to children and animals: but at that moment I really hated Mouro. It seemed like I was a POW, captured by Italian fascists, on a forced march up a mountain, chained to my fellow men. Next year I will book Tenerife instead, I thought.

Meanwhile back on the mountain, it seemed that we were near the top, as beyond the next steep slope was only blue sky. At the final stretch, a traffic jam was building up near the summit, as the large Dutch party were trying (with some difficulty) to create some steps in the virgin snow. We almost caught up with our lead party of Patrick, Aran, Andy and Chris who had been cracking on at a decent pace.

As we plodded up the steep slope, Howard shouted out "Stop!" At this point that Howard was struggling with the altitude and felt dizzy and nauseous. I was so grateful that we could stop for another rest and others were feeling the altitude effects; maybe it wasn't just me.

After six hours, and 1,300 metres elevation from the hut we reached the top. The view was amazing, we could see the French Alps to the north west basking in the clear blue skies, whereas the Italian Alps to the south were partially covered in a blanket of clouds. It was a difficult to believe that we now were higher than the carpet of white fluffy clouds beneath us.

After some celebratory photos and group hugs with Howard and Jerry, Mouro began to make some grunting noises and pointed to a rock to the left of us. Then we realized that this wasn't official summit. We were on a plateau ledge about six feet of which was a large cornice hanging over a cliff, which I warned Jerry about as he was walking across it during the photos. Everybody left their sticks in the snow and we set off for the actual summit that was another 50 metres along an annexed ridge jutting off on a tangent.

The "summit ridge" did not seem much higher than we were now, but we had to traverse along a rocky ridge that varied between 15 feet and 6 feet wide in places. On either side of the ridge was a terrifying, sheer drop on both sides: I had never seen anything like this before. At this stage of the game I was tired, thirsty and a narrow, icy ridge with a 1,000 metre drop on each side was not a welcome prospect. Unfortunately, the ridge was littered with lots of large icy boulders that had to be scurried over (or around). At the far end of the ridge was a statue of the lady Madonna. It was the definitely the time and place for religion.

The obstacle to the summit ridge was a large icy boulder blocking our path. To get round this bloody obstacle you had to grope your hands around the top of a boulder (coated with ice) and shuffle your feet along the ledge. The ledge was both dangerously narrow and horribly exposed and the drop from the ledge was a several thousand feet of pure oblivion. All we had to do was balance along the ledge that traversed around a large icy boulder: it was eight feet in diameter, *but it seemed like eight miles*. The challenge was extreme, as there were no hand holds and the shape of the boulder was awkward and protruding thus preventing the prospect of leaning forward to stabilise the balance. The crampons and axe were (ironically) useless on this section, and the only insurance policy was that I was roped up to three other guys (three knackered Brits and Mussolini) – who were anchored to… precisely nothing. Basically, one slip, and four of us would plunge over the ledge into an abyss of biblical proportions. Nevertheless, we were still roped up following Mouro along the ledge –there was no choice but to follow.

Once we had balanced across the ledge, there was no place to rest along the end of the ridge. There was a lot of chaos and shouting on the staggered summit which we could now clearly see 15 metres in front. There were approximately five separate groups at the edge of the ridge, and they all were roped up in their individual groups. The Dutch lads began moving around the ridge like excitable ants, criss-crossing each other to get to the Madonna statue. Beyond the Madonna statue was the end of the ridge and another drop into nothingness. Amazingly none of the ropes were attached to the rocks so the people clustered together had no protection. Our party (Mouro, Howard, Jerry and me) was still queuing up (still roped up) almost level with the summit which was occupied by a crowd of approximately twelve climbers. The queue for the end of the summit ridge came to a gradual halt for ten minutes and my view was completely obscured by Howard's rear end as he crouched on a rock above me. The view to the left and right was not much better. I had ten minutes for my eyes to fully absorb the horrifying drops of several thousand feet to the east and particularly the sheer drop to the west. At that point I would have paid an undisclosed sum to sit down on the ridge boulder, to rest and beg for some water like an exhausted Labrador.

Amongst the strange Euro confusion on the top I could see the faces of our advanced party and shouted out for a photo – Chris and Andy were sat down on the crowded summit watching the Euro chaos.

"Chris! What's it like over there?" I shouted.

There was a slight pause. "I'll tell you later!"

Knowing Chris for twenty years I realized that his answer was loaded and he wasn't enjoying the spectacle. In contrast, Aran was standing up, hands-on hips (Napoleonic style) and he seemed to be thriving in the ridge summit chaos, shouting at the Dutch guys.

"Clip your ropes on to the karabiners on the rock, otherwise you'll all be fucking history."

The guides decided to join in the shouting in French and Italian, and it seemed that everybody was now shouting. It was all Greek to me. Perhaps this was sowing the seeds for Brexit. I'd seen enough. I just wanted to sit down somewhere, take some photos and find a place to push Mouro off the top – so I joined in the shouting. After a while the shouting stopped, with no noticeable change in behaviour from the Dutch students, but people seemed to feel better. I decided to take some action myself, and shouted to Howard (who was in some sort of silent trance at this stage) to tell Mouro to turn back down the ridge to the plateau where our sticks were parked.

"You want to turn back?" said Howard. Somehow Mouro understood these words in English, and I can only guess he was familiar with the expression. Mouro shrugged and pointed in the opposite direction to Lady Madonna, and now Jerry was in the lead as we retraced our steps back along the ridge.

There was no getting away from it, we had to get off the ridge by going back across that ledge again. It was the only way back (*there's no other way*, as Blur once sang). This time we had a larger audience as we were now at the front of the queue off the stepped summit. It was Jerry's turn first, and he began to shuffle around the ledge gripping his arms around the boulder like a teenager on a first dance at the prom. Jerry was moving so slowly, he seemed to be smooching with the boulder, rather than traversing around it.

Mouro, spotted this hesitancy, and had at last found his tongue "Jerreeee! Move your feeta!"

Jerry eventually got around the boulder and when the rope got tighter I knew that it was my turn. In my terrified brain my wobbly legs began to shake, but when I looked down my legs didn't seem to wobble (*maybe this was because my trousers were a bit baggy*). There could have been a small disco going on those trousers, but when I moved my feet I became fearful of catching my crampons on my baggy leggings, which would have been a certain trip and fall. The main problem was that I was roped up to three other people and if I fell off the ledge then I would drag them down with me so the chances of a fatal fall were quadrupled. As I shuffled slowly around the ledge I also became aware that one of the straps on my crampon was loose and trailing precariously… at this point I decided that looking down at my feet wasn't the best policy so I focused my eyes on my groping hands on the icy rock as I shuffled sideways around the ledge. It wasn't pretty to watch, although I was pretty terrified. When Howard followed, and I could see from his contorted face, that he was not comfortable as he shuffled around the ledge of death: I did think at this stage, "Shit, I'm roped up to him and he's going to slip!". Howard did the business and I saw the look of relief on his face as he stepped onto the wider section of the ridge. Three of us were done and one to go; I didn't even bother to watch Morou's ledge traverse as the rope train began to move down towards the plateau in penguin style crampon movements.

We'd made it.

During our brief rest to collect our walking sticks Mouro provide some rather belated advice when he lifted Jerry's ruck sack and said "Jereee much too heaveee!" and I refused to begin the descent until taking some group photos with the summit as a backdrop.

And so we finally began to descend. It was initially steep. We took great care taking steps downwards, with toes pointing at angles and leaning back (*Lemmy* style). Mouro was leading the way down a little quicker than his three tourists in tow. The problem was that we were all still roped up and Mouro wanted to increase the pace: as his rope was so tight he was pulling Howard forwards. We were going quite fast anyway – but it wasn't fast enough apparently as Mouro started to speed up.

Once we reached the deep snow it became a battle to regain balance and maintain the pace that Mouro was setting. Inevitably we began to lose our balance dozens of times. When one person slipped at least one other got pulled down by the rope into a domino effect. The soft snow made a cushioned landing, but made it difficult to get back up quickly: the novelty of falling down in the snow began to wear off.

 The rush to the hut was causing more of a hindrance than benefit. Mouro still wasn't impressed with the number of stops we were having due to individual falls in the snow. Skiers whizzed down the slopes at breakneck pace. My head was feeling better now that we were descending and found myself with new energy (and more oxygen). Mouro's cavalier pace was causing falls – and creating stoppages. Even Howard was getting annoyed with Mouro who appeared to be getting some sort of kick out of pulling Howard over. Things got a bit tense when he tried to continue this policy and I asked to be de-roped in Anglo Saxon terms as I was beginning to feel part of a P.O.W march again; also being in the middle meant getting pulled from the front and back. De-roping was now an option as crevasse danger had passed. Jerry who had slipped many times on the way down took a nasty fall face-first catching the ice axe strapped to the back of my rucksack. The next day Jerry's face looked like a cross between *Mick Jagger* and the *Elephant Man*.

Two things struck me on the way down (apart from Jerry's head): firstly, I couldn't believe we had walked up this many slopes: secondly, how noticeably easier it was to breathe when we reached about 2,800- 3,000 metres.

It took about four hours to descend from the summit to the hut. For most of our group it was our first real Alpine climb, and our first 4,000 metre mountain completed. The textbooks classification of the Gran Paradiso as a "basic snow/ice climb" in view of the lack of crevasses and technical ability required and some say it is one of the easiest peaks over 4,000 metres high. There is no doubt that it would have been physically much easier without the deep snow. After a total of ten hours walking through deep snow it was certainly the highest and hardest walk we had ever undertaken.

With the passage of time the memories are selective. It is easy to forget the long, soul eroding ascent through deep snow. However, memories of the chaotic and vertiginous summit and the magnificent views of the Alps from high altitude do not fade so easily.

When we reached the mountain hut, Mouro was sat at the bar wearing a big smile. Suddenly his miserable persona had vanished and he had decided to become happy (possibly in expectation of a tip).

"Garree, would you like *Coca Cola?"*

"No thanks," I said, shaking my head. Maybe I'd like to say that I told him to fuck off; but that would be fictitious, and after all, this journal is supposed to be non-fiction. Consequently, I did a very British thing and complained bitterly about Mouro's antics, not to his face, but outside the hut to a sympathetic audience. A good moan is good for the soul: it works for me anyway.

And so after shedding a few layers of clothing I went outside in my T-shirt to bask in the sun for a rest. My water bladder had finally defrosted so I was belatedly able to drink some water. Then it was time to leave the hut and descend the final stage to the bottom of the mountain. As we trudged down the well-constructed path, the snow was melting on the ground and I felt the warmth of the sun under the big blue sky: It seemed like a million miles away from the perilous peak we had left behind,

The Gran Paradiso was our first great alpine experience. As Jerry rightly said, we would be dining out on this one for some time; and we did, and *that ledge* will never be forgotten…

SNOWDON - 6ᵀᴴ OCTOBER 2007

A few months after the Alps trip, I sent an email to all of the usual suspects to see who wanted to walk up Snowdon at the weekend. The usual suspects consisted of Chris, Howard, Aran, Gordon, Andy, and Jerry. Luckily, I received two positive replies from Aran and Andy - who had both been on the Alps trip and were still on speaking terms with me. All three of us were in denial about our middle aged status, so we talked-up our levels of fitness. We were ready to walk across the Snowdon horseshoe ridge. A slight correction here is that I had only told Aran and Andy that we would do Crib Goch and Snowdon summit and back down again which is a normal trip for walkers who want to do some scrambling on Snowdon. They didn't know that they would be tricked into completing the entire horseshoe at Snowdon.

The Snowdon Horseshoe is a magnificent ridge walk that takes in the peaks East Ridge of Crib Goch, Pinnacle Ridge, Crib y Ddysgl, Snowdon summit, the south east ridge of Lliwedd, and finally down to the Miners Track of Pen y Pass. Incidentally, if you cannot pronounce all of these names then you are obviously not Welsh – and therefore you should watch your back in Llanberis: seriously, as far as ridge walks are concerned, it cannot be rivalled by any of its counterparts in England or Wales.

Despite all of the above, Snowdon is often shunned by the purist - and you can understand why: crowds of tourists clog up the main mountain paths on the east side; on the west side it gets worse as the train belches out clouds of smoke on its way up to the summit. Yes, that's right, somebody decided to build a railway track up the Snowdon summit – on the dark side of the mountain. If that's not enough of a scar on this beautiful mountain, then there's the horrible café just below the summit (described as a "disgrace" by Prince Charles). Apparently the café has been rebuilt and it represents something less hideous – but don't expect the Taj Mahal.

In summary; if the swarms of selfie-taking, North Face tourists do not spoil the experience, then there is a high chances that natural intervention (the clouds) will ruin the summit views anyway. To be honest, the weather is the main spoiler. The reader is probably thinking that I am taking all the fun out of Snowdon and my answer to that is; it wasn't me who built the bloody railway and that pathetic café.

Like most experienced walkers we planned to stay away from the tourist routes to the summit and choose the less direct routes which involve more effort: most people don't like "more effort" hence the railways and cafes – business is business I suppose.

We had chosen a clear sunny day with good visibility in order to appreciate Snowdon in its full glory. I was still based on Warrington in 2007 and it is equidistant to the Lakes and Snowdonia (2 hours by car, each way). Unfortunately, everybody else seemed to have the same idea of going to Snowdon, on the same day that we chose. We parked up at Pen-y-Pass, at 9.00 a.m. which meant that we had to park another mile down the hill, moving further away from our intended start point… and getting dangerously near to the Pen Yr Gwyrd Pub.

Our planned route was Pen y-Pass, East Ridge, Crib Goch, Crib-Ddysl-Snowdon, Lliweddl, South East Ridge. The most dangerous part of the day was when the three of us stretched our stiff legs and plodded up the A-road. We were literally walking on the A-road because there was no pavement. The cars roared down the hill towards us, and now that I had stepped out of my car and breathed in a lung full of fresh Snowdonia air I was a country person that hated cars; "get back to your urban jungle," I muttered, as a succession of speeding cars wafted past me. Whilst plodding along the tarmac of the road, I was genuinely afraid of these *iron horses*. My assumption was that all the drivers were texting whilst driving. Yes, welcome to Britain, the sun had come out and everybody was going crazy. Eventually we reached the starting point on the Pyg track, next to the car park and we were beginning to think we had chosen the wrong day.

The Pyg track is always busy, but once the path forks and the tourist traffic flows onto the left for the Pyg track, whilst the path to Crib Goch goes off to the right; we took the right path - which was fitting for the smug trio. This was where the walk really started because we knew that the next section was a steep path that would eventually develop into a scramble. Before the scrambling section, to the left we could see some fantastic views that opened up of the cwm to Lliwedd and the north east side of Snowdon; the mountain had given us a tantalising glimpse – a bit of leg.

The scramble up to the east to the ridge of Crib Goch became gradually steeper until we had to use our hands and feet to climb upwards. This was great fun; there was enough exposure to encourage firm handholds and secure footholds but at the same time there was confidence in the familiarity of this route that we had climbed before. The three of us made great progress going up the east side of the mountain. Looking upwards there was a vast canvass of blue sky above us with the morning sunshine on our backs. I was thinking at this stage that the scene was set for a great day on the mountain. Aran and myself had successfully managed to talk Andy into coming along on the Snowdon trip. Andy had done these peaks before but nowadays he was into high adrenalin sports such as ice climbing, paragliding and incredibly long bike races - mountain hikes just didn't provide enough excitement for Andy.

"Andy, when is the last time you did Snowdown ?" I asked, looking to my left where Andy was scrambling.

"Last time I did Snowdon, I walked up with the paraglider on my back, and I jumped off the top of Crib Goch," he said with a grin.

"Jesus Christ, *I* can't imagine doing that," said Aran.

"I'm not sure I could take the initial step off the ridge – and then put my life in the hands of polythene and poles," I said.

"I wouldn't trust myself flying a paraglider," said Aran.

"You just need to find the thermals to stay up as long as possible," said Andy, casually as if he was describing something simple like tying his shoelaces.

"This is a boring question.... but can you get insurance for that type of activity?" I said.

"You're right, that is a boring question. Insurance companies don't like to insure risky events."

"I guess that sums that it up." I said, and we changed the subject.

I only recently discovered that there are nearly always easier paths to the right. During dry weather and good conditions, like today, it was a perfect scramble with a good selection of hand holds and footholds directly to the top.

When it became very steep, I stopped my idle chit chat and began to concentrate on the climb. My senses were triggered and I became a bit more aware of my own mortality; one slip and it would be messy. Yes, I started to get my wobbly disco legs especially when my feet were tentatively finding footholds. The east side leading up to Crib Goch is a steep scrambling section that deserves some respect. But considering that this was my third ascent; I was feeling confident - there was always a good foothold to find. It's fair to say that the fear factor definitely fades away with a familiar scramble; no surprises equals relaxation.

On reaching the top of the east ridge of Crib Goch we sat and admired the views. One hour of puffing and panting was rewarded by a few minutes of spectacular panoramic views of the Crib Goch ridge, and the mountains of Snowdonia as a backdrop. Despite the magnificent mountains to the west leading up to Anglesey, and the rugged Carneddua mountains to the North, the immediate challenge of the ridge to our south was the view that captured the focus of our minds. The long arête has plenty of exposure; in places its very narrow, but incredibly straight and level.

On this glorious day the ridge had turned into a bustling highway of scramblers. Inevitably, traffic jams were expected, because all walkers move at their own individual pace that they are comfortable with and maintain at least three points of contact. The last time I did this ridge walk I saw a local walker, strolling along this ridge hands in his pockets, smoking a cigarette, skipping from rock to rock – following his dog. In an extreme contrast, I've seen some novices cling to the ridge like limpets, slowly inching their way along the spiky arête.

While I was gazing at the views, Aran and Andy set off along the ridge in a blink of an eye and left me behind. I was still fiddling with my digital camera because my memory card was full (these were the days before smart phones) so I did some "overtaking" on the ridge to catch up. The ridge deserves some respect and I breached this rule by messing around with my camera (whilst walking the ridge) resulting in nearly tripping at one stage and narrowly avoided the direct route off the mountain.

The main rule on the straight narrow section is to keep to the left of the crest whereas the drop to the right is "sobering" and reminds you exactly where you are (just in case you've forgotten). I remembered traversing this ridge with Chris a few years back and was amazed to see Chris tackling the right side of the ridge, gasping and dripping in sweat. The right side has a sheer drop and limited footholds.

I had finally caught up with Aran and Andy at the section of the ridge known as the Pinnacles. The Pinnacles are three distinctive camel humps from a distance, but close up you realise there are ways over them: either through them or round them. This section was adrenalin fuelled. When the ridge broadened out at the approach to Crib y Ddysl – a dome shaped ridge in its own right – this provided a good lunch stop. "Lunch stop" was an overstatement, it was more of a nibble on sandwiches and a quick drink of water to keep up our strength. We knew that we would try to leave our rest spot before the next bunch on ridge walkers caught us up. In the meantime we could watch the other sweaty scramblers complete a difficult stretch that we had just done – with a healthy degree of smugness.

"Were we really going that slow?" said Aran, with a mouth full of tuna sandwich.

"No. We were going much faster than that," said Andy munching on his nuts and raisins.

As the other scramblers got nearer, we quickly packed up the remains of our snacks and stuffed them into our small rucksacks. We had travelled lighter today as the alpine experience had taught us not take tins of beans up mountains. If our rations ran out we would have to draw straws to decided which one of us would be eaten first; or even worse we would have to visit the Snowdon summit café.

As we ambled along the ridge, as Snowdon summit loomed in the distance; looking majestic in its perfectly formed domed shape. It was quite strange because everything was going to plan; but then again, how could we get lost on a ridge?.

Looking forwards there was nobody in front of us; momentarily granting us the honour of having the ridge to ourselves. Then we noticed the railway tracks to the right and the crowds trooping up the popular Pyg track to our left. Just below the Snowdon summit the crowds started to form as people spilled out of the train at the railway summit stop. On the approach to Snowdon, it remained a beautiful clear day and the dark shadowy mountain looked impressive from all angles. When we reached Snowdon's dome shaped summit there was no shortage of strangers to take a team photograph: I would guess at around a hundred people.

After taking in the summit views, we decided to take a vote on whether to complete the other half of the horseshoe (the south east ridge) or to call it at day and limp down the Pyg track with the *Berghaus* brigade. The ballot was confidential; what happens on Snowdon stays on Snowdon. For the sake of reference we'll just say that a person called "Andy" voted to terminate the horseshoe walk at this point. So the climatic summit event had resulted in the procreation of another ridge, previously unannounced to Andy. Fortunately, the ballot result of 2-1 was favourable for Aran and myself - and the South East Ridge was our next challenge. I was pleased about this, because it had been a glorious day so far, and there was the potential to ruin it by being overambitious with extended routes.

We continued with the horseshoe by leaving the summit on the south side of Snowdon. We negotiated our way down through large scree slopes, mostly marked by a loose zig zag path, but undefined in places. We started off carefully but began to pick up some speed. This is where our walking sticks proved to be invaluable (especially if you've got a dodgy knee). We continued a rapid decent down the south side to intercept the Watkin path.

We headed up towards the east ridge scramble up to Lliwedd. This was the best part of the horseshoe. The sun still beamed down, but not quite as fierce; It just had that pleasant warming effect. Conditions were dry and I just felt very lucky to be on the horseshoe on this day. We moved across the dry, warm rock taking the direct route on the crest up to the lofty twin peaks of Lliwedd, and at this point noticed the fearsome drop to the left.

The Snowdon massif has many personalities, and many different perspective. From the South East Ridge we gazed at the dark outlines of Crib Goch and Pinnacle Ridge which deserved to be captured by the camera once again.

"These views never look as good on the photos," said Aran.

"The first rule of photography; buy a decent camera!" said Andy, who had more pixels than Aran and myself combined.

"You can talk about cameras all you like. There is no substitute was witnessing this horseshoe with the naked eye," I said, getting on my high horse.

"Look at those clouds casting blotchy shadows over the mountain, capture that."

"Looks menacing," said Aran as the shadow of the clouds crept across the mountain.

We had the south east ridge to ourselves. Most people traversing Crib Goch call it a day at Snowdon and ignore the rest of the horseshoe. We only saw about half a dozen people on this entire eastern ridge. Sssssshhhh! Keep it quiet otherwise they might extend the railway or build a *Little Chef* on Lliwedd.

The horseshoe finally ended with a long trudge down the knee jarring steps to the ground level besides the lake, and I was quite knackered at this point. Aran and Andy were also burnt out. It had been a long walk. An epic. It had been Physically and mentally exhausting. Let's face it; a wrong move on the horseshoe could have resulted in paying off my mortgage earlier than expected.

"If your knees are not aching at this stage you are probably very young, or a liar," I lamented, as we walked down the hill to the *Pen Y Gwyrd* pub. The first pint of real ale didn't touch the sides, and then second went straight to my head. Andy recommended a café called "Pete's Eats" in Llanberis. I didn't have high hopes for eating in Llanberis because I had been to some frosty places in this town before, but I was so hungry I didn't really care.

Pete's Eats is a restaurant in Llanberis which Aran and Andy had visited twenty years ago. The décor was quite "earthy", and very informal. It had wooden floorboards, long wooden tables and lots of walkers chatting noisily. This meant that we didn't have to remove our boots, which was fortunate; after nine hours of intensive walking my socks had melted into my skin and the removal of boots would have triggered a public health warning. After what seemed like years, our plates of chili con carne had arrived. I was so hungry I was thinking of ordering another main course.

In the car, on the way back home. The day had been absolutely first class and wondered to myself if there would ever be a better day spent walking in the hills? I remained hopeful.

LANGDALE VALLEY - 20TH NOVEMBER 2007

Wainwright's chosen route to walk the Crinkle Crags is to set off from the Old Dungeon Gill, up the Pike O' Blisco by walking along the Crinkle Crags and then Bowfell summit (via the climber's traverse) and then back down the valley for fish and chips before catching a bus home to domestic bliss. Apart from the fact that buses and chip shops are becoming extinct (we won't comment about domestic bliss) we decided to choose a route up one of the three Gills, to Crinkle Crags.

Admittedly, we were still basking in the glory of the Snowdon horseshoe walk in October; as if by miracle, Aran, Andy and myself had actually completed the actual route that I had planned from my armchair. Now, as an atheist, I don't believe in miracles, because the scientific explanation is usually more convincing, but we had completed an ambitiously long mountain route because of three main reasons: the weather was perfect for walking because it was dry and there was no wind; secondly, we had moved fast, with light loads with not too many stoppages and; we didn't get lost.

Despite the unqualified success of Snowdon, we could not persuade Andy to venture up the lakes as he had other high adrenalin activities on his mind. Aran was keen to travel up from London to go on the walk and Warrington based Howard was also up for it.

It always seemed to be me who did the planning for these walks, and I was very happy to choose the routes. Nobody seemed to complain about the routes; not to my face anyway. During some evenings, I enjoyed dipping into various walking books (especially *Bob Allen* books on Lakeland Ridge Walks) and reading about 'new' peaks and ridges. There were so many different walks and routes to ponder over. Sometimes, I would google around the internet looking at walking blogs to check out the different experiences and the condition of various scrambles such as Lord's Rake, Jack's Rake and Striding Edge. The walk had to include a mountain, a peak, or several peaks. I found that the most enjoyable walks were those that enabled you walk up to the high ground, and stay up on high ground for the longest possible time. Circular routes were logistically the easiest. Once I had a plan that was it - I was like a dog with a bone. Unfortunately the plans were usually over ambitious and the routes were rarely completed, due to three reasons: firstly, poor weather and visibility on the mountains; secondly, slower mobility due to varying levels of fitness and stoppages; thirdly, poor navigation – erm, you know - getting lost. Almost all of our walks were plagued by at least one of these three factors. Of course we didn't help ourselves; we fixed dates to walk the lake routes regardless of the weather forecast and none of us could claim to be a competent navigator. Regardless of the downsides, we all enjoyed just getting outdoors and having some good banter during the day out.

The route that I planned (over several cups of tea and digestive dunkies) was starting from Langdale valley, moving up to Crinkle Gill, Crinkle Crags, Bowfell via Climbers traverse, back down the band to the Langdale valley.

From Dungeon Gill Hotel we headed west for "the Band" on the eastern side of the Langdale Valley. Instead of going up the Band which is a great shortcut onto the Crinkle Crag/Bowfell peaks (and the Climber's Traverse), we skirted around to the left and followed the mainstream that was heading west. We had a choice of three Gills to follow;- Browney Gill (left) Crinkle Gill (centre) and Hell Gill (right). It seemed a bit too early to go for the "Hell" option, although our combined "sin" count must be quite high by now. As we set off up the hill via Crinkle Gill, fully decked out in Winter gear we had our usual chat about gear and equipment. It usually started off with serious questions about what gear we were using, but once the cards were the table, it ended up being a battle of sarcastic remarks, and poorly disguised wit.

"Hey Aran, nice waterproof trousers," said Howard with a glint in his eye.

"Thanks. I really them. They're from *Decathalon* you know. Thirty quid, good fit and nice and light."

I looked at my waterproof trousers which were of the old baggy variety.

"Yeah, quite stylish, you're a dedicated follower of fashion…" I said

"*We seek him here, we seek him there, his clothes are loud, but never square…*" sang Howard giving me sideways glance.

"I really must get some of those trousers," I said after the singing had stopped.

We followed the stream upwards as it cut its way into the foothills of the Crinkle Crags, until it opened up into a small valley of its own. The valley was narrow initially and gradually it widened out. The higher we climbed, the more ice could be found on the grass, and the harder it became. As the sides of the gulley got steeper the clumps of grass became the only handhold as we sought a higher position up the valley walls. The walking sticks did the job, but only just. There was a really steep drop down into the narrow valley and I remembered the story of an accident not far from here where a man had fallen down a Gill and whilst we waited for rescue for several days – he managed to keep himself alive with a packet of biscuits. Luckily, Aran had brought along some custard creams, so we were lucky – in case we got unlucky.

"How far to the top?" said Aran.

"Shouldn't be too far now," I said, but in truth I didn't really know. As Wainwright used to say, "It always takes longer than expected to reach the top." Wainwright was usually "wright", as the clue is in the name itself.

Eventually, the Gill opened up to reveal a waterfall in the centre of an impressive amphitheatre. You'll have to take my word about the engaging scenery as I managed to lose my camera on this walk. The slopes leading up to Mickle Door looked almost too steep to tackle from a distance, but as always, it looked easier on closer viewing. So far, as planned, we were sheltered from the westerly winds that were forecasted as gale force. Before we reached the scree slopes of Mickle Door (not to be confused with Mickledore on Scafell) we had to pick our way across a boulder field where we experienced the first real snow and ice of the day.

The scree slope marked our route to the summit, which lay in between two buttresses of the Crinkle Crags. This bit was a struggle as the scree was loose and the rocks were icy, so it was easy to stumble off balance. The walking sticks could not purchase any grip on this loose surface and there were a couple of slips. As we neared the peak we were beginning to feel the force of the gale - in contrast to the quiet and windless Crinkle Gill behind us. The head-on westerly gale was now bombarding us, making a tremendous roaring noise. Eventually, we used the right hand cliff wall as something to hold onto, and edged our way up along the side of a small rock face wall to the summit.

This dramatic ascent was more difficult than expected and the intermittent thunderous gale ripped through us, inflating our coats which pushed us precariously backwards. It got worse near the top when we were forced to go on all fours to avoid being pushed over. Mickle Door is an aptly named gap in the ridge between two impressive buttresses that mark out the rocky peaks of the Crinkle Crags. Today, this gap was the doorway to a powerful wind tunnel.

Once we got to the exposed peak we bore the full brunt of the gale. When I looked round I saw Howard walking behind me, coat and trousers bubbled up - looking like the *Michelin* man. Aran wasn't looking too cheerful either - I sensed that getting battered by this wind was not mentioned in the brochure.

The wind was so loud that we couldn't hear each other unless we shouted from two feet away. I noticed that Howard had a red plastic bag tied to his walking stick.

"Why are you carrying a red inflatable condom?" I shouted. But it was no use - there was no way Howard could hear me whilst wearing the full protection.

At last, we were on the Crinkle Crags, but we could see nothing. There was no view to reward our efforts - we may as well have gone to *Tesco*. The visibility was blocked by low cloud which intermittently cleared every few minutes to show some way forward to the north, keeping the valley to our right (the east). The only problem was that I had based our route on being able to see the landmark of the Three Tarns just before Bowfell - and now we had limited visibility. I could not afford to make a wrong turn, but didn't share the navigational worries with Aran and Howard; there was enough to worry about.

We continued walking north across the Crinkle Craggs to Bowfell peaks, but we were stumbling along, drunkenly. Occasionally the horizontal icy rain or hail would be lashing into our faces. Unusually, the ridge was the least enjoyable part of the route. Aran spotted a groove in some rocks to shelter behind, and we rested for ten minutes for food and drink. There was an instant boost in the morale of our trio. It was a good move by Aran; we really needed that break.

We continued to stumble along the rocky ridge and thanks to a break in the fog we could see the Three Tarns, just below the path leading to the Bowfell summit (Hallelujah! We were now on the right track). Next we descended down to the broad sloping ridge known as "the Band" and we began looking for the Climber's Traverse, I decided to walk ahead to try and spot the path that skirts across the eastern side of Bowfell, but I managed to lose Howard and Aran in the process. I was conscious that we had taken an hour longer than planned due to the strength of the winds, and was trying to make up for lost time – by getting lost. I waited and turned around like an excitable puppy waiting for its owners.

On meeting up we found the Climber's Traverse and the walk changed again completely. Now in extreme contrast again we were totally sheltered from the gales on the Eastern side of Bowfell. There was no wind. We continued along a narrow ledge traversing around Bowfell and this is where the fun started.

To the left, a steep rock face of Bowfell - cathedral like in places. To the right was a steep drop; casually referred to in walking books as "some exposure" where every danger is understated. The traverse was quite spectacular as the ledge hugged the side of the mountain; it was almost 'Tolkienesque' in places.

To our surprise the path was covered in snow, and littered with frozen puddles; it was tricky going in places. We instantly regretted not bringing our ice axes and crampons because the walking sticks became a false sense of security; they could steady your balance, but were unlikely to stop you slipping over the edge.

The steep buttresses of Bowfell to our left separated us from the summit, but we couldn't find the route to the summit so we continued along the legendary Climber's Traverse. It was a conveyor belt that was difficult to step off.

Howard was lagging behind, and I couldn't work out why.

"What's up?" I asked, turning around watching Howard walking tentatively forwards.

"My feet are slipping on the ice. These boots have no grip," said Howard.

His feet were slipping around on the ledge. I could see he wasn't happy with this section. The traverse got worse when the track degenerated into a sheep track or just vanished in some places where a tricky jump was necessary. This should have been a clear sign that we had followed the path too far and that we had missed the left turn up the Great Slab leading to Bowfell mountain.

Aran and I did what most other friends would do buzzing on the adrenalin of exposed ridge paths and ignored Howard's discomfort - clicking away with our cameras and marvelling at the impressiveness of the famous ledge. However, we did offer token words of encouragement to see him through, "Just a bit further Howard" "nearly there" and the classic…"you'll be alright mate". Howard saw through the bullshit and was asking questions like "are we nearly there yet?" and rather annoyingly, "do we know where we're going ?" . In the interest of team morale I fobbed him off with a reply of "yeah, not much further now."

In reality, there was no obvious route to the summit of Bowfell from the Climber's Traverse, despite being able to see the Great Slab to our left.

The clock was ticking and time was running out - the Climber's Traverse had petered out and we soon found ourselves on little more than a sheep track. I pushed ahead to see if there was anything round the corner, and in front of me could only be described as the "Lonely Sheep's Traverse" (the story of my life). Meanwhile, behind me, Aran was eyeing up a scree slope on the northwest face of Bowfell as the access point to the summit (just to the right of the Great Slab). Howard decided to get off the Climber's Traverse and started a careful descent down into the valley.

It was now one hour until darkness - so there was no room for error. Aran was keen on going up the scree slope to the Summit and coming down the Band. This was probably the fastest route (although the north west facing scree slope looked icy) but this meant that Howard would be left on his own to descend into the steep valley.

After a quick debate we decided to revert to the ethics of "going up the mountain together and going down together" and we left the path and make our way down the steep slopes. Aran chose a direct route down across a field of large boulders to diagonally intercept Howard's descent. I foolishly agreed and followed, and we began to negotiate our way across the large icy boulders (some of them were the size of small cars). During the hopping process I must have dropped my camera and Aran ripped his designer leggings. When I say 'designer' I mean *Decathalon*, but they looked good to Howard and me, so we'll stick with the 'designer' tag.

Meanwhile back in the New Dungeon Gill Hotel after a couple of pints of "*Black Sheep*" we became wise and philosophical about our losses.

"The mountain gives and the mountain takes," Aran surmised.

After the second pint paranoia started to kick in... had God punished us for abandoning Howard on the mountain by taking away my camera and ripping Aran's leggings?

****

THE COLEDALE ROUND – 16TH FEBRUARY 2008

"Everyone must know the feeling of triumph and pride which a grand view from a height communicates to the mind" (Charles Darwin 1836)

It was 8.00 a.m. Saturday morning as I drove up the M6 to the lake district. My two passengers Aran and Jerry had gone through the usual Friday night ritual of heavy drinking and limited sleep. In those days it wasn't known as "binge drinking", it was simply known as "the weekend".

We arrived at the car park just outside Braithwaite village on the Winlatter Pass (B5292) at 10.00 a.m. The car park was full up, so we joined several other cars by parking on the grass verge. I was thinking that the Coledale Round is obviously a popular walk despite its location in the quieter part of the North West Lakes.

One of the random walkers that I had spoken to on a previous walk had recommended the Coledale Round as "a decent ridge walk." From the comfort of my armchair I plotted the route which was basically; -Braithwaite - Grisedale Pike (791m) - Hopegill Head (770) – Whiteside (743) Sand Hill (756) – Eel Crag (AKA Crag Hill) (739m) – Sail (773m) – Outerside (568m)- Style End (447m) - Braithwaite The Grid ref. NY 227238.

Did you notice that I included the grid reference here to impress you? But this was of no consequence because the route finding was simple, and the weather was very kind. With just a few steps up from the car park we were presented with fine views of a newly planted forest to the north and Bassenthwaite Lake. It never fails to surprise me that in the Lake District how quickly airy views can be attained by the slightest height gain. The narrow path from the car park quickly broadened out into a well-trodden motorway (Okay, that was a slight exaggeration - it was a wide path). The winter sun, combined with the hazy mist gave the distant fells a dreamlike appearance. This was perfect weather, no wind or rain, skies fairly clear and everything else in our favour. The natural environment was clearly in a good mood today; even the grass consisted of a springy texture on the lower slopes which helpfully assisted our ascent up the Sleet How ridge towards Grisedale Pike.

During the ascent to Grisedale Pike we entered the usual discussions about hiking gear. I was travelling light with a very small rucksack containing two litres of water, food, a torch, and a GPS (the latter was for just for show). The rest of the stuff I actually wearing; light Gore-Tex boots, waterproof leggings (*Decathalon*) to prevent any suntan and a new lightweight coat. Gone are the days of carrying huge bulging ruck sacks containing all of those "just in case" extra layers of heavy clothing. After our two day trek through deep snow in the Italian Alps where we punished ourselves by carrying excessively heavy loads, we were now trying to travel Alpine style; very quickly up and down the mountain (in the same day) with the bare essentials in the rucksacks. Part of this process involves scrounging off your pals who are unwittingly carrying the heavier loads (effectively becoming two legged camels). Aran was sporting a new yellow fleece (*fell hopper* brand) to break away from his *Decathlon* only policy. Jerry, a warm witty and polite chap had long hippy style hair and had remained faithful to his old, tried and trusted gear (possibly from the 1970s) and somehow managed to complete walks without the aid of designer label clothing. We did point out to Jerry that his waterproof cagoule was no longer waterproof as he had washed it around two hundred times since its purchase date. Jerry did not disclose the year of purchase, but he seemed quite content with his gear, and the mild weather was not likely to test it today.

During the long climb towards the Grisedale Pike we made ground easily and stopped to take pictures of the panoramic scene unfolding in front of us which I will try to describe; Coledale Beck snaking its way along the Coledale Valley way beneath us; to the east, we could see the layers of neighbouring ridges such as Newlands and Buttermere; In the far distance, the dark and moody Helvellyn range; but most of all - Skiddaw dominated the landscape to our south east and Bassenthwaite to the south west.

In this part of the lakes was a lot of mountains to feast your eyes on. Whilst posing for pictures we suffered the humiliation of being overtaken by some very old people. Today, I would not refer to these people as "old" as that would be ageism - which is a crime punishable by death - but they were "mature people" progressing well into their sixties.

The usual way to respond is to overtake these people, at a breakneck pace, but this seemed inappropriate in the relaxed and hazy ambiance. Given that Aran was discussing his favourite subject (sex) I decided a safe distance from the earshot of the well-heeled elderly people was to our advantage. For some reason Aran continued on the same subject at increasing volumes as we slowly overtook the old folk. It might have been a cry for help.

Grisedale Pike was the largest climb of the horseshoe and for the rest of the walk we maintained the height by staying up on high level ridge, with only relatively small ascents to the other peaks. I wished that all walks could be like this.

Whilst making the slight descent from Grisedale, the steep sided Hobgarth Crags could be seen. The Hobgarth Crag formed a "u" shape of impressively steep cliffs. These Crags host a rare vegetation clinging to its scree laden walls that is of apparent interest to botanist. When we got nearer Hopegill Head, we realised that there was a sheer drop for the walker to the west of the ridge over the Crags which would be a risk during poor visibility. I wondered if the botanist would actually climb these cliffs for a closer inspection of rare bits of weed; did that make the botanist more, or less crazy that the climbers?

When we reached Hopegill Head, a view of the Whiteside ridge (see picture) opened up before us; it was one of the longest ridges I have ever seen in the lakes. It seemed to go on for ever. The Whiteside ridge is a spectacular arête, although fairly level, it's almost one mile long with steeply sided slopes on either side of the narrow path. The crest of the ridge had a well-worn path which was perfectly formed. Now here's the thing - the path is wide enough to give you the security of "feeling safe" but narrow enough to give you the feeling of exposure (depending on how near you wish to walk to the edge). The view to the west was the much less severe landscape around Cockermouth up to the Irish Sea. The view down the eastern side of Whiteside is an awe inspiring drop of the Gasgale Crags down into the deep, narrow valley of Gasgale Gill with Liza Beck at its foot, following the line of the ridge (between Coledale Hause and Crummock Water). I just couldn't take my eyes from the awesome drop down into the Gasgale Crags. This was a genuine use of the word "awesome" as people use this word as a response to almost every banal occasion nowadays, "do you own a car?" and the reply would be "awesome." This is almost as annoying as the increasing use of the word "period" to mean that something has finished - another example of irritating "American-English" dialogue. I could go on, and mention that nowadays we don't "contact" people we …"reach out" to people as if somebody is in need of rescue - being swept away down a fast flowing river: rant over.

"This path would be really dodgy during strong winds – it's too narrow," said Aran as he strode tentatively along the path.

"I don't think it could be done in strong winds. There's no margin for error," I said, concentrating on my feet.

At the far end of the Whiteside Ridge, facing south we were greeted with a fantastic view of Crummock Water. On this occasion the lake was shimmering brightly thanks to the reflection of the low winter sun. Whiteside ridge (facing Crummock) was an ideal place for a rest before we set off back along the ridge to complete the other half of the round. When we sat down, and admired the views, there was a rare quietness in the air. There was almost complete silence apart from the distant sound of a trickling mountain stream. The *West Wycombe Wamblers* (as Aran and Jerry like to call themselves) soon got comfy, and stretched out on their backs in unified silence. I must mention here that Aran and Jerry are overworked, underpaid (and "over holidayed") teachers, and it didn't take long for them to enter rest mode - and fall asleep.

For me - relaxation is a stranger, so I busied myself checking the map, dutifully switched on the GPS and tried my best to keep Aran and Jerry awake by constantly babbling on about anything in particular. Initially this policy worked until I reminded the teaching faction that there was no bell to signify the end of "break time." It was so relaxing lying on this grassy sun drenched ridge, you could close your eyes for just a few more minutes and happily die peacefully here… guys, we have to complete the walk within seven hours before darkness.

We eventually restarted our walk and retraced our steps across the Whiteside ridge to approach Hopegill Head and the second part of the Coledale Round. We turned east just before Hopegill Head to reach Sand Hill and the Coledale Hause; our eyes were fixed upon Eel Crag (AKA Crag Hill) and the path dipped down steeply into the valley the prospect of a steep climb up the shadowy west face of Eel Crag. There was a temptation to climb the adjacent Grassmoor but time was against us. From a distance the steep climb up to Eel Crag looked a bit tricky and it was tempting to follow the tourist route that loops round to the South side of Eel Hill for a gentler ascent. That would have been too easy. The Wainwright way was to take the more energetic route and go straight up the steep side of Eel Crag and one might question his motives when there's an easier route next door to it. Was it the sheer adrenalin rush obtained from scrambling up steep scree slopes without handholds or was the poor old blighter just suffering from sexual frustration? Regardless of his motives, the old man was right; the direct scramble is the way to go. For most of the scramble we had to contend with loose scree and my clumsy feet managed to dislodge some stones, causing a few small avalanches down the steep slope towards Aran.

"Watch out, rocks!" I shouted as I triggered another mini avalanche.

I heard Aran mutter something from down below, but at least he was okay.

Jerry was scrambling ahead of me so I also had to contend with small stones trickling down towards my head. This was the only real scramble of the entire Coledale Round so I can't complain too much. There were a couple of quiet moments near the end of the scramble, where extra care was required when the hand holds disappeared. In some places I was forced to cling onto the strands of vegetation, and put my faith in weed to get higher.

So far, this walk had been running very smoothly - unlike most of our other walks. There was a strange ambience of calmness, a dream like surrealness about the whole day, epitomised by the hazy visibility. We hadn't got lost, the weather was sunny with an occasional gentle breeze; the paths were clear and dry all along the horseshoe, and the ridges had well-trodden paths. Navigation was easy as we could see the route clearly in front of us and we hardly looked at the map, the ridges were wide enough and even the grass was springy. It would have taken a great deal of inventiveness to get lost on these clear paths with the full horseshoe route for all to see. There were no kit problems, or people having the wrong gear, or arguments about the chosen route or pace being too fast or too slow, or too many photo stops. We continued on the narrow ridge that lies between Sail and Causey Pike thankful that there was no westerly wind to contend with. To the east, we saw some spectacular views down into Newlands valley (…that was another walk, for another day).

We merrily plodded on and after one third of a mile we passed Sail, and there was a clear junction in the paths and the choice was to continue on the high ridge to Causey Pike or to take a left towards the traverse path from Sail to Outerside. We took the left which departed from the main ridge and this was a clear shortcut to Braithewaite. The path must have been something formed by the miners in need of a pint at the end of a hard day grafting down the mines. Such minor scars on the landscape are completely forgivable in the whole scheme of things; nothing much comes between a thirsty man and a pub. We gradually descended the hills getting nearer to the "real world" with a tinge of sadness. With Braithewaite village now in view we took another shortcut that was a beeline to Braithwaite to cut out the corner of Barrow Gill that looped around.

In these latter stages of the walk our minds became focussed on the pub. We had really earned the beer and were in genuine need of refreshment. It was also at this stage that Aran and Jerry began to sum up the merits of a day's great walk, brilliant choice of routes, perfect weather, and the company… yeah above average, I suppose. The addition of Whiteside onto the round was considered as a masterstroke, and although these may not have been Aran's exact words, you get the general gist. I did receive a lot of praise for planning the walk and of course I revelled in this, and decided to seek more accolades by confidently stating that that the best pub in the entire Lake District is apparently the Coledale Inn, based in Braithwaite I might add. The pace quickened again at the thought of sipping the finest ales in the finest pub. In reality we didn't have a clue where this pub was and ended up at the Royal Oak P.H. in the middle of Braithwaite village, a small a maze of narrow side streets.

This pub was pretty good. It was warm, friendly and had some decent real ale. In fact the Jennings bitter was fantastic. Everything was perfect after a long day on the fells…
"Wait a minute, we can't leave Braithwaite without going to the best pub in the Lake District."
We creakily raised ourselves slowly from our chairs. Our stiffening legs were reluctantly called into action. We went off in search for the Coledale Inn and those extra three hundred yards walking seemed like three miles.
On entering into the brightly lit Coledale Inn we lumbered up to the bar. Two large smelly dogs lay slavering on the bright blue carpet. We stood there on the psychedelic carpet, tired and blinking under the bright lights and the red velour chairs.
"Guys, this is either an old people's home or a 1980s disco," said Aran; no stranger to 1980s discos. We exchange looks and were about to turn round and make a quick exit, when a voice came from the bar.

"Don't worry about the reserved signs… come right in and sit down!"

We sat down obediently and choked down our second and final pint of the day.

THE SCAFELL RETREAT - 29TH MARCH 2008

Weather Forecast for 29th March 2008

"Hazards. Blizzards, severe wind chill, severe gales, extensive hill fog, heavy rain, ice. Lake District National Park Authority FELLTOP CONDITIONS REPORT from Helvellyn at 11 a.m. on Thursday 27th March 2008. There is wet thawing snow from 450m which increases in depth with height with drifts of 50cm at 900m. All paths above 450m have snow and ice on them. Above 800m layers of wet wind slab snow has covered old, compacted snow, this requires care both in ascent and descent. The cornices that cover eastern facing slopes in the Helvellyn area should be avoided as they are weakly bonded. Full winter clothing, footwear and equipment including an ice axe and crampons are strongly recommended for anyone venturing above the snowline and essential if attempting steep routes. i.e. on Helvellyn. The exits to both Swirral and Striding Edges are still extremely icy and dangerous without the correct equipment. Wind/temperature/freezing level Southwest 40 mph gusts 55mph. 0 Celsius. 900m."

When I saw this forecast it took the wind out of my sails. Despite all this, Aran and Jerry had already booked their cheap train tickets in advance (*Virgin* West Coast trains from London to Warrington), and therefore the show must go on.

The walking books by Bob Allen, wax lyrical about the approaches to Scafell from Wasdale. Here's an example: *"Here you are in the deep valleys, surrounded by mountains but without the backdrop of coast and sea. The landscape on these routes is made up of the immediate tall crags and mountain ranges, bejewelled with glistening tarns, and the more distant pastureland neatly divided by dry-stone walls, dense wood copses, and the expanse of Derwent water."*

On a clear summer's day all of the above is probably on show. In very poor conditions (like today) it's a different ball game - albeit all ball games would be cancelled in these conditions. The prospect of conquering the pikes of Scafell in these conditions was bordering on the impossible.

If you're planning on using this extract from the journal as some form of informative walker's guide then just stop right now. This diary extract is as useful as an ashtray on a motorbike.

The truth is we never even saw Scafell; we saw a few weather beaten walkers retreating from the fells, driven back by the horrible combination of gales, hailstorms, and blizzards.

In the weeks building up to the 29th of March 2008, from the comfort of my armchair ambitions ran wild: Scafell via Borrowdale was easily achievable on a winter's day. Such optimism can be found when sitting on a warm sofa, breezing through the guidebooks whilst dunking four digestive biscuits in my mug of tea, consecutively, without a single loss. From my armchair, anything was possible; it looked oh-so-easy, and I secretly hoped that we could squeeze in some extra peaks en route to Scafell Pike, including Grains Gill and Ruddy Gill, Great End, and Broad Crag. If things went really well we could go further than Scafell Pike and climb the Scafell via Broad Stand and return via Foxes Tarn. Here is the thing; all of these peaks are lined up like dominoes on the map, and they seem to be in close proximity (on the map) so why not bag them all in one session?

Before we witnessed the severe weather, there was another delay event starting on the Saturday morning at 6.00 am in Warrington – the *Next* Sale. This "unmissable event" was announced by my better half on the Friday night, which meant that I was left literally holding the baby(s) on Saturday morning until Kerry returned from her own challenging adventure (I must admit having been to the *Next* sale on previous occasions it is something of a rugby scrum involving lots of aggressive women trampling over each other to grab a £5 pair of jeans.) So the expedition was put on hold for an hour as Kerry returned at 8.30 a.m. We had lost an hour, and it took some explaining to Aran and Jerry that one hour of our hiking time had been sacrificed. A point to note for younger readers is that the *Next* sale was massive in the noughties, before on-line shopping had really taken off shopping was a bit more of a 'physical work-out'. It's doubtful that Chris Bonington's expeditions had suffered delays of this nature but my suspicion is that he had delayed some starts due to washing his hair or trying to settle arguments with Don Whillans.

Admittedly, the main problem of the day was the route finding. There is a time and place to take on a new route; and it's not under severe weather conditions - one wrong turn becomes a crisis. Also, having just one person carrying a map, reading and navigating means the chances of errors are increased. According to anorak books like *Mountain Craft And Leadership*, it's a crime. It seems fairly obvious that when visibility and conditions are very poor it's better to go for the less ambitious route. Ahem, in my defence, I tried to engage in some form of debate about the route and options available by sending emails containing various routes prior to the walk, by placing maps strategically on the passenger seats (only to be sat on and put away in the glove compartment or used as pillow on the way back home.) I guess, in reality map talk is boring - after all it's a day out and not a geography project. Who wants to discuss route options and severe weather warnings during the two hour car journey up the M6 (in a car full of maps) when you can discuss world affairs, politics, music, relationships, and joy of shopping at *Aldi*? Throw in a couple of intellectual teachers, and you've got a great talking shop. Let's face it the English are great talkers and we just love a debate, but rarely get round to actually doing anything. Anyone who has read Cornelius Ryan's "*A Bridge Too Far*" will appreciate that we Brits are quite capable of planning logistical cock-ups on a grand scale and to continue with the Arnhem theme we also landed a couple of miles short of the drop zone, got lost and never achieved our objective – but revelled in the glorification of failure.

The drive, from Derwent Water follows the pacey Derwent River for miles cutting through the wooded Borrowdale Valley alongside Castle Crag, is impressive. Judging by the speed of the river Derwent, supplied by streams pouring down from the flanks of the fells, these parts had been getting more than their fair share of rain and snow.

We arrived at the Seathwaite village car park at an embarrassing 11.00 a.m. We got booted up and donned extra layers of attire and were ready to finally start the walk at 11.30, yes that's 11.30 a.m. on a short winter's day. Just as we were about to pay the £5.00 parking fee, Aran got 'tapped up' by a salesman lurking next to the pay-and-display box who was flogging national trust membership for £55 a year. I pointed out that we would need 11 visits a year to justify the fee - and for me this would be grounds for divorce as my wife will only walk with the aid of shopping bags. But the smooth talking salesman threw in a couple of freebies (two small rucksacks) into the deal and Aran was quickly reaching for his wallet. I have to say (for the sake of world peace) that regardless of the parking fee, the National Trust does some great work in the national parks and it's very difficult to criticise their existence.

Finally, we headed south, down a country lane along towards Seathwaite farm, and after about 2 km of trudging down a tarmac B-road two things struck us; horizontal rain at 55mph and the realisation that other walkers were clearly cheating by driving past us to park at Seathwaite farm and cut out 4 km of unnecessary walking. The look on Aran's face was a real picture as he scowled at the cars parking near the farm: without a doubt next time we would cheat too. We quickened our pace to keep warm – it was bloody cold.

The country lane took us straight into Seathwaite Farm and then on to Stockley Bridge following the River Derwent all the way. On the bridge we looked down at the fast flowing river and the energetic feeder streams leading into it. The Lakes is one of the wettest parts of England and the Scafell range is the highest and wettest part of the lakes sitting in its position as the first barrier from the south westerly winds ripping across the Irish sea: if you have been, you get the picture.

We headed for Styhead Gill by taking a right turn just past Stockley bridge although we wouldn't be able to see the Gill until we had found a way through the Aaron Crags on the West side of the valley. Grains Gill is accessed due south. There seemed to be so many Gills around here, what could go wrong?

The horizontal rain continued to hit us head on - that is literally head on. There was no way of avoiding this wind as our route was mainly southward bound until we reached our final destination of Scafell, and then we could turn around and enjoy the wind on our backs on the return northwards to Seathwaite. The question was: if the weather was like this at the foot of the sheltered valley what would it be like higher up on the exposed peaks?

It always seems to be cloudy here, and today was no different. The cloud base seemed to be around 700m, which covered the peaks sitting above the ridge roof of the valley.

As we trudged along the river path towards Grains Gill, we met a solitary red faced walker, who stopped briefly enough to tell us of harsh conditions on the peaks; blizzards and soft snow underfoot. It wasn't clear whether his rapid descent was due to the wind pushing him northwards back to Seathwaite or just that he was in a hurry to find a warm fire and a pint of *Jennings* beer.

Due to the poor visibility, the only object that could be photographed was Stockley bridge:

the low cloud was sitting on top of the rim of the valley and we could barely see Glaramara to our east, and none of the Scafell's to the south could be seen. We could only guess that somewhere to the south was Great Gable.

The map had indicated a fork in the two Gills around a very prominent conical shaped mountain, called "Seathwaite", which is more prominent than the map had indicated. The left Gill was Grains Gill and right Gill was Styhead Gill. We crossed over on the left hand side of the river Derwent and ascended the most prominent Gill on the left. I was thinking that this was Ruddy Gill so we began a steep ascent next to the rocky stream, which had over flowed and soaked the grass a few metres either side. It was a tough ascent that got steeper and steeper; a couple of times we nearly got blown over backwards (and it was a long way down). The nearer we got to the top the more the wet vegetation became a handhold necessity, and another reason to soak the gloves. I looked to my right and saw Aran striding up the hill, seemingly breathless: he was pace setting, and I became suspicious of some foul play.

"Have you been working on your fitness?" I said, gasping for breath.

"Yes, I have," said Aran, not gasping for breath.

Aran had confessed he'd been getting fit over recent months. He found a resting place behind some rocks just before the top of the valley, and it was a good place to stop before we took on the full force of the gale driven rain. Ever the optimist I decided to put my safety harness (ready for Broad Stand) instead of a vital map check, it was too cold to stay still for long and do both. I was expecting to see Esk Hause and a crossroads of paths, next to Styhead Tarn but when we got to the top we could see nothing… no paths, no tarn, just boulders, virgin snow and mist. We had climbed to the top of a steeply walled valley, and found a non-descript, broad ridge of higher ground.

On the top, we were truly out of the valley and at the mercy of a terrific head on gale. Aran went to the left (north) towards Glaramara. I tried to shout him back but he couldn't hear through the racket of the gale; I tried to wave him over (which was a difficult task when I was holding on to my hood). We went to the right (south) and saw three people sheltering behind a rock, they made their way towards us, and we had one of those strange broken conversations in the midst of the gale. They had aborted an ascent of Great Gable and now looking to descend via Ruddy Gill (although they had walked past it by 1 km) so we unwittingly directed them down Red Gill (admittedly we were also convinced it was Ruddy Gill). That would be a steep descent, and not a Gill to descend unless you were absolutely desperate. I did stress this point but the three guys just nodded politely, satisfied with my answer: It was the blind leading the blind. Just before we let them get on their way one of the three (I only remember that he had a southern accent) made some comment about his wet feet and asked if he could swap boots with me, and it was just then that I lost my footing and fell through some soft snow and into a mini Tarn up to my knees. The southerner, apologized unnecessarily my fall in a very British manner, and at that point the three men made their way to the precarious drop into the valley. They didn't get a mention on the national news so we can only assume they got down okay.

At this point we continued our search for the path but to no avail; the mist came down and the situation became quite desperate. Aran and Jerry just wanted to keep moving somewhere, regardless of direction, as we were becoming soaked by the relentless rain and hail. All of us had stepped into the snow covered wet marshy ground at some point or another – wet feet on a freezing winter's day was not good. The surface snow was masquerading some small shallow tarns that we kept stepping into, and this was becoming an ordeal.

The rain had managed to drench our waterproofs and somehow find its way through the leggings, gaiters and everywhere. We went further to the north east to see if we could pick up a path, only for me to step into a bog (knee deep). Now both feet were wet, cold, and were beginning to squelch. As we squelched on, there was still no path to be found. We had been searching for this non-existent path for about twenty minutes now, but in these conditions it seemed a lot longer, and we were back where we started. Aran was getting worried about Jerry whose 100% woollen hat was now 100% soaked. We needed to move, keep warm, and set off in the right direction. I was reluctant to make a move until we had agreed some sort of plan whilst we were together behind the sheltered rock. The heavy mist intermittently lifted to provide a sneak preview of new views (but no landmarks that I could recognise).

All three of us agreed on one thing: we had to get off this mountaintop and quickly. I wanted to go west and head for the corridor route, and Jerry just wanted to get out of the gale: we were all in agreement on the last point. As we were sheltered from the gale I could hear Aran mention the option of going back down the way we came up; but I wasn't keen because it would be a really steep descent. "Go West!" I suggested (after all it had worked for the *Village People*). On leaving the refuge of the rock, we headed west, in a direction that would find Sprinkling Tarn or the Corridor Route - or at the very least find an escape route back into the valley.

But during this half hour period of getting battered by gales, hail and lashing rain it had a negative impact on our morale, composure and... group unity. I've been in this "lost in the storm/mist/gales" situation before: on previous occasions and each time I felt miserable, disorientated and was in some form of mild panic. The first time on the Eigua horseshoe in Wales where the mist was very thick and had to follow the sound of a stream going back into our valley (without a compass), the second time on the Carneddua (Drum) again where the visibility was about thirty feet (this time, with a compass) and we went down into a valley. Now this was the third time where I had become lost in the mist. This time, I had my GPS to guide me in the right direction. I drew some confidence from the GPS, and I knew which direction to go in and very roughly how far we had to go to skirt round the north end of the valley to the Sprinkling Tarn, and other landmarks. Aran and Jerry were without map or compass and were in the hands of me, an armchair mountaineer leading them into a hellish gale in the middle of nowhere on a bleak mountaintop.

Despite taking the wrong Gill I was convinced that if we headed west we would pick up Sprinkling Tarn and the Corridor Route or at the worst the descent down Styhead Gill. If we missed all of those we would bang into Great Gable (an easily recognizable landmark). I held the GPS device up in the air, like a beacon of hope, and headed straight west.

Aran and Jerry followed for a few minutes in silence, and then I could hear some grumbles of concern, but like a true comrade I ignored them and plodded on at a faster pace. The guys weren't happy: the terrain was marshy and very damp and there was no path or sight of a landmark on my map. I was getting angry with myself that we had gone up the wrong Gill, but at this stage I was 100% confident that a straight line west would work, but wasn't sure how far out we were. I was desperate to see a landmark, a tarn - preferably Sprinkling tarn. After ten minutes we came to a wide stream crossing with deep snow on either side and Aran and Jerry were now deeply upset, and grumbling loudly.

Still, getting battered by the head-on wind, the instinct was to head northwest, follow the gentle slopes towards the valley so then the wind was more side on. The mist cleared and we could immediately see the Borrowdale Valley to our right (north) and the way we had come. Eureka! a bit of relief: now we could see an exit down the valley, and a landmark.

The relief was shared, and all of a sudden it wasn't so bad. Aran wanted to go down into the valley but we were aware of precipitous north facing cliffs and would have to pick a clear and safe spot to descend. I was still trying to keep a straight west getting battered by the side wind, and Aran and Jerry were walking level with me but were gradually (north west) going down to find an entrance to the valley and find shelter from the fierce wind. A kind of north west-west compromise was reached and we were now scattered out in a line.

The sacrifice was giving ground of a few hundred metres but we gained something by dipping below the cloud - we needed a rest and a bite to eat. We actually found the path (not visible from the foot of the valley) leading from Grains Gill into Ruddy Gill and decided to stop for something to eat. We compared notes; we were all soaked, cold, hungry. Worse than this, we all had cold and wet feet and hands; we really needed to change into a dry pair of everything. My new sealskin gloves which had got wet during the scramble up Red Gill were still soaked. Jerry tried to squeeze some water from his woollen head gear, and I wanted to remind him that woollen clothing had been popular with Victorian mountaineers until the invention of something called nylon and polyester.

Another three people came down Ruddy Gill and stopped to chat. One man whose dark blue coat and leggings were shiny with dripping water spoke through the small gap in his hood which almost covered his entire face.

"We've been up on the Corridor Path, turned back at Piers Gill as the path vanished in the snow. Then a blizzard had created a white out and the path could not be seen."

I was immediately jealous that they had made it to the corridor path. These people were certainly more clued up than the three we had seen earlier and they had all the right gear.

"…we brought our crampons but the snow was too soft…"

They described the deep snow, gales and blizzard conditions at length, and then a woman spoke for the first time.

"Well, you know, this weather *was* forecasted," she said as a matter of fact, with a hint of I-told-you-so: her two male companions nodded and looked at the ground sheepishly.

We nodded glumly in poignant recognition that we had all seen the weather forecast and ignored it. The conversation ended as there was no further point in talking as if today's weather was a freak event. Well, I suppose that God loves a trier.

Now we knew that the Corridor Route was off limits and pondered what to do next. Our new mentors suggested that if we went up to Sprinkling Tarn, Styhead Tarn and back down Styhead Gill it would be a realistic walk given the conditions. This was good advice.
We climbed up the Grains Gill/Ruddy Gill path with the dramatic Ruddy Gill to our right. It was nice to move on an established path, and today was a day for established paths, modest distances and realistic targets (…ahem).
Once at the top of the Gill we crossed over the stream and followed a path leading to Sprinkling Tarn and began to enjoy a stretch of walking noticeably sheltered from the strong southerly winds. So much to the extent that we began to enjoy this stretch: it was on a level, and it was easy walking. Spirits raised further when we continued west to meet Styhead Tarn. Styhead Tarn is almost like a high level "base camp" for the several mountain ascents such as Great Gable, Pillar group, or Scafell Traverse walks.
Great Gable stood impressively beyond Styhead Tarn, and for a few minutes we looked up in admiration at the visible bottom half of the impressive dome shaped mountain with its snowy slopes: we were all thinking the same thing, "shall we?". No - we wouldn't have time it was almost four o'clock already (only two hours of daylight left). Any remaining ideas of climbing Great Gable were wiped out when we rounded Styhead Tarn past the stretcher box and felt the force of that horrendous southerly wind accompanied with lashings of hail. That was the final signal to turn round.

Then we descended Styhead Gill (on the right side) and trudged back towards the car. Well, it was a "reccy" after all. We did well to cover some distance under difficult circumstances, and had only met eight other walkers during the whole day, all of whom were either lost or aborting Scafell, Great Gable or whatever their objectives were.

When we got back to the car we were all cold and soaked to the bone, despite having layers of waterproofs. Jerry's waterproofs looked like they had seen some action over many years of use and he disappeared for a long time in the public toilets: later he returned carting his wet underclothes underarm, wearing his outer layer only. The journey home reflected the weather as the M6 at Lancaster was closed due to flooding. Jerry had done the right thing by taking all of his soaking clothes off to replace them with the dry layer that he had left in the car. When we were back in Warrington we began unloading the car - I picked up a dripping glove from the boot. Aran and Jerry unloaded their gear from my car to make their way to the station.

"Jerry, you've left your black glove in the boot of my car!" I shouted as Jerry and Aran walked away carrying their rucksacks. Jerry turned round and smiled.

"It's not a glove, those are my briefs!" said Jerry, prompting Aran to burst out laughing. My facial expression was a mixture of dismay and disgust, and I dropped the wet briefs onto the pavement and tried to dry my wet hands on my trousers. I had suddenly gone off Jerry, he had crossed a line.

THE SCAFELL RETURN - 6th SEPTEMBER 2008

Planned Route: Seatoller farm-Stockley Bridge, Grains Gill, Ruddy Gill, Sprinkling tarn,

Styhead tarn, Corridor route, Broad Crag. Return the same but via Taylorforce Gill.

I really don't know why, but six months later we decided to return to 'the Scafells' again. The weather forecast was wind 40-50 mph, strong to gale force, heavy rain, north east winds, and low cloud (500m). Does this sound familiar?

I was clinging on one optimistic note – we have done this before and we have done the "lessons learnt" analysis. But why?; for the mother of god would we be looking to repeat the "Scafell Retreat" see (last chapter). The grim reality was that we were going on this day as the train tickets had already been booked. We had decided that during our last Scafell trip we had built up some good knowledge of the Borrowdale-Styhead Tarn area and all we needed to do was to get on the Corridor path and up to the Scafells: it would be like stepping onto a conveyer belt.

In attendance, we had the usual suspects; Aran, Jerry and me.

This time, we also had a new addition. We'd always requested the company of Mr. Andy McKay, but without success. Could Andy be tempted by the draw of the Scafells? ... Er no, Andy was already booked into a 100 mile plus bike ride on the Sunday, so he wasn't going to do both: so, Andy sent his better half - Lesley, a true walker who liked walking and …reading maps (hallelujah! A map reader). There was (and still is) no real enthusiasm for map reading amongst the three of us, so Leslie was a welcome addition.

We parked on the approach to Seatoller Farm in a familiar setting of torrential rain and low cloud. We were getting geared up quickly outside the car and managed to get wet before the walk started: welcome to the Scafells.

Believe it or not, we set off with a map, but no compass (I left it on the front seat of the car) and a GPS. As we reached the farm we took full advantage of the public toilet facilities to avoid the embarrassment of toileting "al fresco" on the Corridor Route.

We headed north along the valley of Borrowdale, following the Derwent River. Gradually we started to ascend Ruddy Gill and Grains Gill with a new determination. Last time we tried to do Scafell from Borrowdale we got hammered by head-on gale force winds and turned back. This time the only issue for us was how bad the conditions would be on the peaks.
Early signs weren't good, as people were tramping down Ruddy Gill towards us: mostly looking wet, miserable and defeated. We asked the first group we met if they had reached the summit and were given a collection of reasons why they couldn't get to the Scafells; wind too severe, conditions too harsh, maybe another day, etc. We had no alternatively - but to prepare our own excuses in advance.

As we were midway up the Gill, we were faced with a new type of delay we hadn't experienced on previous walks. Firstly it was Aran who managed to leave the path by a respectable 20 metres or so and began to get down to do his business. Unfortunately, there wasn't much coverage so we kept a look out.

Near the top of Grains Gill, we met more groups of people who had been driven back by the weather: there were some claims of 100 mph winds on the mountain tops. We scoffed at these highly inflated estimates and carried onwards. We were expecting stronger winds at Styhead Tarn, but we figured that the Corridor Route would be sheltered until we got to the main battering on the peaks.

At the top of Ruddy Gill, Aran and I were the first two over the narrow crossing point over the stream - using our walking sticks to useful effect. Then we waited on the other side of the stream and began to watch Lesley and Jerry crossing over. Lesley was hesitant but made it across okay. It was quite a tricky river crossing as most of the steppingstones were under the water, so they were quite slippery. Then came Jerry's turn: we all waited and watched from the other side of the river shouting words of encouragement - because we were experts now. Along came Jerry who stopped half-way across, didn't fancy it, and there was a bit of a drum roll, a lot of wobbling… then splaashhh! Jerry fell into the river sideways with cartoonish inevitability. It was only two feet deep, but deep enough for an extremely cold bath. Jerry flapped his arms about in the icy water and staggered out of the middle of the river like a drowned scarecrow towards the riverbank. The fall was both funny and shocking in equal measure. Remarkably, Jerry seemed the least concerned, as he straightened up and refused the offers of helping hands. It was even more surprising that Jerry mentioned that he was not wet to the skin: amazingly Jerry's old 1970s waterproofs turned out to stream proof, if not rain proof. The selfish part of me (approximately 100%) was seriously worried that we might have to turn back if Jerry was soaked to the bone. Like a true Brit, Jerry was ready to carry on. God bless him. We continued the walk wondering what would happen next.

We met some of the strongest winds of the day at the stretcher box (near Styhead Tarn) where we took a half left turn, rather than a sharp left and mistakenly joined the Corridor Route to Wasdale Head. We realised after about twenty minutes and doubled backed to the stretcher box, where a mountain rescue man was perched behind it, waiting for the next call out. We asked him sheepishly which way to the Corridor Route and he dutifully pointed us to the path (bloody difficult to see if you asked me). Yes, we all agreed it was a perfectly easy mistake to make (although, he probably thought we had the potential to be his next call out).

As we started on the corridor route, it really felt like we were finally in the Scafell mountain range. Most of the quitters had already passed us on Grains Gill and now we had the corridor route to ourselves. The good thing about the Corridor Route is that you can just plough on without the worry of getting lost. So, as we started to pick up a bit of real pace someone shouted "let's stop here for lunch": It was a sheltered spot, so why not. Thirty minutes later the four of us got our rucksacks on and continued down the well-trodden path. We had been walking for ten minutes, and we came to a halt. "Stop! I need to go…" shouted Jerry as he perched behind a rock not too far away from the path.

And so we continued along the twisting corridor route which was sheltered from the worst of the wind. It was getting quieter, with hardly any foot traffic. We passed one or two weather beaten walkers, but it seemed that only a few had actually reached the peaks. Before we reached Piers Gill, we saw a path going upwards. Everyone thought this was the one leading to Scafell Pike. Lesley got the map out and we all stared at it in wonder. I decided that my memory would be a better navigational guide.

"There is only one path in this area leading up to the Scafell peak," I lamented, as it would have been rude not to join in a map debate. It was only later when I looked at my detailed map that I realised there were two main paths: one up to Broad Crag and the other to Scafell Pike. The ascent up to the peak was a hard slog, and we zig zagged up through the loose scree slopes. Progress was slow. As we were on the last stretch we entered into a wind tunnel. The wind was hitting us head-on and it became difficult to keep balance. This was tough, as we were already knackered from ascending the loose scree slopes. We had now lost sight of Lesley and we waited for about ten cold minutes at the side of the wind tunnel clutching on to the walls for balance. Something was wrong and Jerry managed to find Leslie who could be seen crouching down. My immediate thought was "Oh no! Not another crap stop," but I realised that Leslie was holding her map, trying to locate a clear path ahead. The problem we had was that there was no clear anything ahead, it was low cloud with visibility of about fifteen yards at this height.

On the top, there was a level boulder field hosting boulders the size of washing machines which we had to navigate across to get to the summit. This was awkward and the north west winds were very strong and loud so we couldn't communicate with each other unless we were right next to somebody. All of this made progress really slow and I began head off in front with a ten yard gap trying to find some sort of path.

At last we reached the peak! The highest point in England! Aran and myself stood on the highest point, walking sticks held aloft in act of celebration. We'd done it! We'd managed to conquer Scafell Pike. As we were congratulating each other there was nothing but low cloud all around us. Then Lesley piped up "Where's the trig point?".

The handshakes continued, but less vigorously this time. At this moment of self-doubt I noticed an empty tin of beans on a rock and cursed at some inconsiderate camper who had refused to move their trash off the mountain.

"No, Scafell Pike has got a proper trig point; this peak must be Broad Crag or Ill Crag or some other bloody place, the Pike must be further to the north."

Slightly deflated, we began to plod northwards: but could we find the real summit of Scafell Pike in fifteen yard visibility in gale force conditions? After a while we realised that simply heading north in 5 metres visibility on top of the Scafell range was probably not a good idea. Then we then gave up and went west to find our way back. Before we knew it we became disorientated and had a brief stop and then held a crisis conference behind a large rock. Annoyingly, we couldn't find the gulley that we had ascended (which was about 15 metres wide) so we decided to go back to the peak of Broad Crag to try and trace our steps to the way we came up. Everyone was cold, wet, tired and there was a bit of panic creeping in, as we had an hour before darkness and wanted to be off the peaks by then.

Wainwright could find his way around the Scafell range blindfolded. He loved Scafell.

I wondered what Alfred Wainwright would make of our situation.

"Mountains generate mist and look naked without their delicate white shawls. The effects are often startling, often incredibly beautiful, always interesting, never frightening".

"Dry mist is a charmer, wet mist a snare, but neither is the cause of accidents, but clumsy walking is."

The old man had no fear of mist. Hhhmmm.

Meanwhile back to Broad Crag peak; despite the peak not having a trig point, this peak was recognised by finding the same empty tin of beans on this summit that we had spotted earlier – who needs GPS? Broad Crag offered us some shelter as found a gap between two slabs. We assessed our situation: we had a map, a GPS (for direction, but no O/S positions), no compass (that had been left in the car), two of us were very wet, and one was visibly shivering. Aran always carried spare clothing (all with decent designer labels!) and he dutifully handed out a dry hat and gloves to those in need. We all agreed that the descent was west, but couldn't understand why we could find the path. Lesley quite rightly thought we were on Broad Crag, and the steep Crags illustrated on the map were nearer to Scafell, so in theory we should find a route down the mountain.

Wainwright did not believe in carrying a compass. Unlike us his knowledge of the mountains was immense.

"I never carried a compass, preferring to rely on a good sense of direction".

We began to inch our way down from the ridge. I ventured ahead trying to pick out the best route down. At one point we scrambled down only to put the brakes on when we saw a thirty foot cliff immediately below us. In the mist, we couldn't even be sure how big the drop was as we could only see about 15 metres in front, and this meant edging our way further forward and trying to peer over the cliff. It was morale shattering to go back the way we came to try and find another way down further along the ridge. After doing this several times, I was starting to get worried as we were burning up time and energy: I wondered how many cul-de-sacs we could visit before we simply burnt out of energy and darkness descended.

Again, we tentatively walked down around 20 metres from the top and went level for a while looking for a sensible route down. As we plodded across the ledge the atmosphere was quite tense amongst the group: at this point – with almost comic timing – Jerry announced that he needed to go to the toilet. Perhaps this was a good luck sign, or perhaps we been granted more time to look around us to look in the opposite direction, but as the mist cleared a bit we spotted a route down. Plus the visibility had now improved to 30 metres.

We continued our descent on the grassy slopes and then we began to follow a stream: this was a real morale booster. I had dropped down from peaks in thick mist in Wales on two occasions and on both occasions followed a stream down into the valley. As we began to descend into more gradual slopes we realised that we had got ourselves out of a very dicey situation and everybody let out an unashamedly loud cheer when we spotted the Corridor Route. Lesley was ecstatic. I don't want to over-dramatise this part of the story - but there was sheer elation of getting out of this bad situation. We had just descended one of the UK's highest mountains, in poor visibility on a pathless route. This had been a cross between *Into Thin Air* and *Hound of the Baskervilles*.

Getting lost on the Scafells wasn't exclusive just to our group. The old man Wainwright himself had managed to get lost coming down from Scafell Pike.

"...I learned many lessons that day. I learned never to underestimate the fells; Lakeland heights are small by Alpine standards but they are tough, and the summits are always further than you think."

After trudging down the Corridor Route, it was almost dark. The torches came out as we inched our way down Taylorforce Gill and the walk was prolonged further by the unwelcome introduction of complete darkness. Eventually we found the car (last seen 11.5 hours ago). After pub/drive home/takeaway I finally got home past midnight (after leaving home at 7 a.m.) to be faced with accusations from Kerry ... "Walking until this time? You expect me to believe that?"

Okay - I suppose I am having an affair - a twenty year affair with the Lake District - but not with the Scafells. Next time we will have to approach Scafell Pike on a summer's day – from Eskdale, and not from Seathwaite.

NEWLANDS HORSESHOE - 6TH DECEMBER 2008

Maiden Moor, High Spy, Dale Head (753m) and Hindscarth

On 5th December 2008, I checked out the weather forecast for the next day in the Lake District - and I couldn't believe my luck: Keswick was "good visibility, snow and ice on high ground, wind speed 6mph (no direction)…" my mind had been made up - I was going to the Lakes on Saturday for a one day hike. The only question was who else would join me for a winter hike in the mountains of the Lake District?

Aran and Jerry were London based and had no plans to visit the Lakes that weekend at short notice, and the other usual suspects like Howard and Chris couldn't make it. I even tried to talk Andy into the winter hike but he already had made plans doing something else: yes, I conceded… it was short notice. The nearest thing I'd done which resembled a solitary hike was the long walk home from town after the pubs were shut, clutching a take-away.

This fantastic weather forecast was an opportunity that was too good to miss: and on Saturday morning, at 7 a.m. I threw my rucksack, crampons and my ice axe into the boot of my car and drove up to the Lake District: on my own – I'm not sure if I've already mentioned that I was going mountaineering, on my own.

It always felt like a religious pilgrimage driving up the empty motorway at 8 a.m. on the Saturday mornings. Any regrets concerning the sacrificed Saturday morning lie-in disappeared on the M6 when the Cumbrian mountains came into view: I became transfixed by the imposing and seductive mountains of the Lake District. Many times I would stray into a neighbouring lane due to rubbernecking at the mountains to my left: trying to identify each one, like long lost relatives. Luckily, the motorway was empty, and there was not a car in sight: I had the whole road and hopefully the mountains to myself. During winter-time the Lakes were usually quiet as the visiting hordes usually visited the lakes in summertime. As I got nearer to the northern part of the Lake District the early morning sun was rising and my spirits were lifted again. When I turned off the M6 and headed west along the A66, I was now within the Lake district national park and I gained an appreciation that it had been transformed by the heavy snowfall into an Alpine landscape. Everything was painted white and the beauty of this winter wonderland was indescribable – but that won't stop me trying to describe it. The dazzling white mountains were contrasted by the cloudless blue sky. Somehow, the perfect blue sky, made the sky look bigger today; it created a vast canvass,- an endless horizon that I couldn't take my eyes off. The morning sun burned brightly to create the perfect day for winter walking in the lakes. I had to think back to ten years back in January 1995, when I had last seen the lakes in these perfect winter conditions, when Howard and I walked up the steep side of Skiddaw. That glorious day was permanently etched in my memory - and in the prologue of this book.

The solitary two hour car journey up to the Northern Lakes had been a little weird. I had always travelled with friends or my wife Kerry to the lakes and chatted en route - so I wasn't used to my own company, and the quality of conversation was not good. During recent weeks I'd been reading Wainwright's autobiography, and although the old man usually walked on his own, there was a method in his madness. I could understand it because he was purposefully seeking solitude. I was not sure If could really embrace the loneliness of a day's walk on my own – and I was about to find out.

I parked up, and without further ado, booted up and set off up the hills. It took thirty minutes before I saw the first hiker. The brightness of the snow was so immense that I used my sunglasses for protection. As I paced forwards with the longest strides that my short legs would permit I was determined to make good progress and there was no need to turn round and check with my fellow walkers if I was going too fast, or too slow. There were no ad hoc stops for members of my party to tie bootlaces or re-adjust rucksack straps. Thankfully, there were no *al fresco* toilet stops. I was my own boss - and I enjoyed the freedom. As I walked on the ridge between Maiden Moor and High Spy the panoramic views were out of this world. I stopped walking just to breathe in the clean air by the bucket load, and slowly exhale then turned to see my trail of footprints that I had left in the virgin snow behind me. I was feeling both liberated and exhilarated at being outdoors in the vast open space, surrounded by mountains. I could see the impressive Blencathra to the north, the magnificent Helvellyn range to the east, the Scafells to the north east. The obvious advantage to walking 'solo' on the fells was the peace and tranquillity: there was a quietness that was only interrupted by the crunching noise of my boot-on-snow. As I crunched along through the snow I became acutely aware of something odd: a quietness that I cannot recall noticing before. There was a stillness out there on the peaks; a calmness created by the absence of the usual sound of the rumbling wind. As I reached higher ground midway up High Spy, I found some more ice patches. At last I could justify getting my crampons on. I sat down on a rock and strapped my crampons onto the sole of my boots in a mild state of giddiness. Today the Lake District was at its best. I made my ascent to High Spy against the mid-day sun. A well named summit with panoramic views of Skiddaw, Hellvellyn, Scafells and the Newlands.

I recalled that Wainwright had mixed feelings about winter walking:

"Snow is a more subtle adversary. It transforms the fells into a fairy wonderland. It is beautiful; beautiful, but treacherous. Snow is feminine, a temptress; when you meet her, watch your step. When her seduction hardens into ice avoid her. The fells are best left alone after frost."

The route I had chosen did not involve much scrambling, and on paper it looked quite safe: but mostly the weather was kind. My crampons allowed me to walk anywhere, without the fear of slipping. Wainwright would have done this without crampons, using only his tweed jacket and walking stick for balance.

The steep ascent of Dale Head was slippery so it was another good excuse to strap on the crampons. You can see that I was desperately trying to justify using my crampons at any opportunity. As I traversed around the circular Newlands route I was beginning to recognise views of familiar mountains, but from different angles and in different conditions. From Dale Head summit I could see Maiden Moor and its steep cliffs, and decent views of the Langdale's (left) and dome shaped Great Gable to the right.

Whilst moving across the ridge between Dale Head and Robinson (Hindscarth Edge) I was tempted to extend my planned route and bag Robinson. A walker with a beard (who I got chatting to en route) reckoned I could fit it Robinson and still loop round to Newlands village. I kept an open mind but when I approached Hindscarth a blister started to kick in, and I blamed it on my unforgiving (crampon friendly) winter boots: my mind was made up - I was going to stick to the original route. Robinson was one of those mountains for another day, I hoped; although when you are young you don't realise that opportunities to retrace old ground are so limited. Okay, so here's the confession: I had been hiking now for around five hours and I starting to become bored of my own company.

On the descent from Hindscarth I could see Ill Crag (from Coledale Round) and could not fail to notice that it was actually lit up by the sunset; this was ironic as the most challenging part of the Coledale Round was being highlighted by a yellow marker pen. The descent of Hindscarth took a long time because I kept stopping to take my crampons off (on rocky bits) and putting the crampons back on (on icy bits) again. This was a routine that I adopted throughout most of the descent: it was time consuming but at least the process stopped me slipping on the way down. Gradually, I became acutely aware that I seemed to be the only person left on the mountain as the low winter sun was rapidly descending and dusk was not far away. I adopted a quicker pace to reflect the urgency and started to slip on the icy patches where I couldn't be bothered putting my crampons on.

On completion of the circular route, I experienced that familiar but inexplicable joy of finding that my car in the same place exactly where I had left it: and it was also job done. Furthermore I was pleased that I had taken a lot of photos of the spectacular winter scenery. The condition of the snow was excellent; dry and firm, and the weather had been perfect. One poignant memory from this trip was the absence of wind on the mountain tops, which is normally prevalent on all mountain hikes. I won't forget that eerie silence only broken with the crunching noise of my boots sinking into firm snow: sounds were more noticeable as my senses were heightened. I expect it did create a calming effect and it was probably more noticeable as I was on my own. The drive back home was a quiet one, and I had to concede gracefully that I had really missed the chaotic company of the usual suspects: Chris, Howard, Aran, Andy and Jerry would have really loved this trip.

The Newland horseshoe proved to me that the Alps and the Scottish hills are not the only options for winter hiking. Back in the office on Monday I printed out the photos of the snow covered mountains on A4 size and put a few of them up on the office wall, for all to see. As soon as people entered the office, they were drawn immediately to the stunning prints plastered over the wall. The contrast of white mountains, blue sky and a blazing yellow sun was very eye catching. Most people asked where the pictures had been taken expecting me to say it was the Alps - almost all of them could not believe that these pictures had been taken in the Lake District, in England.

The Newlands Horseshoe proved to me that I had become bored with my own company, and I was looking forward to inflicting that boredom on somebody else.

KOLACHAL MOUNTAIN - 16TH FEBRUARY 2009

I had the pleasure of visiting Tehran for an eight day duration on business during 2009. Now here's the thing; the city of Tehran is surrounded by mountains, and every morning I looked out of my hotel window and saw snow-capped mountains rising above the cluster of urban city tower blocks.

Admittedly this mountain backdrop created a degree of giddiness and I would guess that any self-respecting armchair mountaineer would fancy a crack at it. In reality "having a crack at it" for the YouTube generation would involve immediate action: going online, and googling the "Albors mountains". Some adventurers might go to more extreme measures and order some books from http://www.amazon.co.uk/. Climbing a mountain is a different game – it takes effort.

I could have looked at these mountains all day, but I needed to get suited, booted and into a meeting with the client. As soon as I arrived at the client's offices the meeting room window had another view of the Albors Mountains. Once again I wondered, if only I could get up there.

It soon became clear that the Albors Mountains were such an imposing backdrop that they could be seen from almost anywhere in the city: they were difficult to avoid. I had been travelling with two work colleagues, Malcolm and Simon. On the second evening we sat in the lounge of our alcohol free hotel.

"Wouldn't it be great to climb up one of those magnificent mountains of the famous Albors range?" I said leaning back on the leather sofa in the reception.

"Yeah, sure," said Malcolm sympathetically, whilst reading the hotel restaurant menu.

"Wouldn't it be great to find a restaurant that serves alcohol?" said Simon smiling sarcastically. Everybody nodded and agreed that this was the top priority for the evening.

A couple of hours later, as we walked to the restaurant (after glancing up at the white capped Albors mountains) I almost walked into a lamppost. The strange thing is that one week ago I'd never heard of the Albors range or the Kolachal mountain before, but now I could think of nothing else, as if it had always been my life's ambition.

I'll let you into a secret, I did actually know about the existence of these mountains before I took the flight from Manchester to Tehran, and just as a precaution I had packed some walking boots and a waterproof coat. During our eight day visit, one of the days was a national holiday so the office was closed; which meant that Malcom, Simon and myself were at a loose end for one day. During the pre-holiday build up I dropped very subtle hints to the local team of people who were involved in our project such as "anyone fancy going up one of those mountains?" Now, also by chance a local guy called Behrooz (from our partner company) was a keen hiker, and he immediately recommended a mountain called Kolachal (3200m) and said he would organise it. The date was set. Kolachal was almost the size of two Snowdon's.

As we set off at 6.00 a.m. I got talking to Behrooz about mountain walking and it was clear that he had a lot of experience (20 years) of the entire Albors range, including climbing the highest peak in the Middle East, Damarand Mountain at 5200m.

Kolachal Mountain was the obvious choice as it was accessible to anyone of a reasonable level of fitness. When Behrooz parked up his car we could see a constructed path winding its way up the mountain. It started at the car park (approx. 1000m) all the way up to the highest base camp (2800m). Now here's the thing, this path was constructed by a group of volunteers from Tehran 45 years ago, and they also planted trees on each side of the path, which manage to survive quite happily right up to the altitude of nearly 10,000 feet. Well, I'm not sure if the trees were really happy at a freezing cold high altitude, but they had survived, nonetheless.

Even more impressively this scheme was a privately funded venture i.e. not government backed. This was a great achievement, and I wondered how many countries in the world had achieved privately funded construction schemes on mountains of this scale. The mountain path also has around six huts en route to the top, nicely spread out at timely intervals. I have never been on a more organised walk. I don't think this is typical of an Iranian mountain and wouldn't like this degree of facilities on every mountain. But nevertheless, a very impressive achievement by a local private initiative that the UK's National Trust would have been really proud of (and would have tried to recover these cost by charging £10 car parking fee). I didn't have my mountain boots on just leather Timberland boots – which were ideal for walking to the pub: What on earth could do wrong? you might ask. I soon discovered that when we reached the snow covered paths (around 2,000 metre) the boot tread was not thick enough, so I began to slip on the paths. The paths were very busy resulting in the snow being compressed by the hundreds of booted feet, and it was melting so the path became something of a ski slope. I got round this problem by either clinging on the trees which lined the path or by taking short cuts across the rougher terrain.

The various groups of local Iranians who built this epic path going up 2800m celebrated their achievement by building a tower on the highest base camp, and on closer inspection Behrooz pointed out that each individual who built the path signed each brick!

I must tell you about Behrooz, who proved to be an excellent guide for this walk. Behrooz was a Kolachal veteran as he had hiked up this mountain countless time. In fact, he had summitted this mountain so many times and when he got married he continued to go on weekend hikes up Kolachal. His wife told him that Behrooz was spending more time on the Kolachal mountain than with her.

Behrooz carried a large rucksack, and I wondered what was in it. The mystery was solved when Behrooz confirmed it was full of food for both of us and a camping stove. Unfortunately there was no room for crampons and an ice axe. So what did I know about Behrooz apart from his passion for food (and the resulting overweight figure)? Behrooz was an easy going character, spoke perfect English and was quite simply great company during the walk. Underneath the mild mannered exterior I sensed that Behrooz was very strict about what to eat and when to eat during the walk, and I obediently followed his instructions. Besides, it would have been pointless to challenge his tried and tested eating and walking routine: and let's face it, I was the newbie, a long way from the hotel, and not far away from the nearest Iranian prison, so I didn't want to cause a scene.

The slow pace for ascent was a critical factor, and the dietary regime made sense but I must admit that the stretching routine that Behrooz insisted upon when we reached the top was new to me. Having said this I felt like a spring lamb on the descent.

The Behrooz formula or walking up the Kolachal.

-Nuts and dried fruit 30 minutes before start

-Lemonade (must not be cold water, he was very strict about this)

-Fruit 30 mins before lunch

-Lunch (on the top) usual carbs and protein.

-Fruit 30 mins after lunch

-Regular fluids.

-Pace during ascent : very steady and even, 1 minute stop every ten minutes.

-On the top : Stretching exercises (...not reaching for the fags)

So, I dutifully followed the Behrooz formula for diet and pace, and this 3,000 metre/10,000 ft mountain felt like one of the easiest walks I have ever done, without any altitude issues. I couldn't believe how relaxing the walk was, and for the first time on a 3,000 metre mountain I felt that I had so much stamina and energy levels in reserve. When we reached the top, I could have quite happily continued onto the 400 m ridge above us covered in snow. As we sat down, not far from the tower memorial, we gazed up at the snow ridge, just above us as Behrooz made scrambled egg on his stove. I had never eaten so well on a mountain walk. There were hundreds and people near the tower, mosque and shops at the end of the official path to the tower. Surprisingly only a few people were heading out on to the ridge above us.

"The summit ridge looks very tempting. Can we do it?" I said.

"We don't have the crampons, and the ridge is not safe without crampons" said Behrooz making direct eye contact with his third egg sandwich.

"Yeah, I guess so," I said, making permanent eye contact with the snow ridge.

I look back to this walk with fond memories, but I always think about the snow ridge that got away... *if only we'd gone up there.* Maybe it is a human instinct that we are never satisfied and restlessly looking for completeness or perfection: when we reach a goal the celebrations are short lived and we are already thinking about the next goal, and so on. I would never consider myself as a perfectionist - far from it - but it is natural to think back and consider… if only we would have done that ridge that looked so close to our stopping point. The grass is always greener…

The mountain walk gave me a very positive experience about Tehran and its people. The politeness and friendliness of everybody I met during the walk was extraordinary, many people were helping each other, including strangers along the paths and people openly shared their knowledge of successful short cuts with strangers. Iranians are very patient and peaceful people, and this image is not reflected in the media's portrayal which is based on personalities and stereotypes - where the characteristics of the political leaders create a false impression of its people.

Unfortunately political turmoil and Government oppression were topics that that the people of Tehran could not ignore and kept rising to the surface on a daily basis. When we finished the walk at the car park, having our final coffee to presumably just chew the fat, Behrooz told me he was not allowed to leave Iran unless he had several documents including a letter in writing from a citizen from another country, like the UK. This seemed to dampen the mood and we finished our coffees in silence and as he collected my empty cup he clutched both empty cups and looked at me expectantly.

"My son has bad asthma and this city is really polluted. My family really need to leave this polluted city of Tehran, for somewhere cleaner – like the UK," said Behrooz, looking at me intently with sad puppy eyes.

Ah, there was no such thing as a straightforward walk in the hills, I thought.

Meanwhile back at the ranch; when we returned to the hotel we discovered that the number of British people we had seen in Tehran had doubled from two to four, as my colleague had spotted John Simpson (BBC) and his camera man drinking coffee in the lounge area.

FRANCE -AGUILLE DU TOUR – JULY (2010)

Day One

I took an afternoon *Easyjet* flight from Liverpool to Geneva airport, to meet Aran who had travelled from London by car. The purpose of the 7 day trip to the Alps was to climb the Monte Rosa and other lofty peaks. By evening we reached the Le Praz campsite, near Chamonix at the bottom of the steep alpine valley. We sat outside a bar and as we drank cold beers we gazed up at the Agui de Midi to the left and the Aguilles Rouges to the right: we wondered about the possibilities of getting onto those ridges. As we watched the evening sun sink beneath the snow crested mountains, darkness descended on the valley to mark the end of the day dreaming session. The snow that clung to the peaks and the precarious slopes was picturesque, but we knew that white stuff is dangerous. At night I shuffled around on the cold hard floor of the tent, trying to get comfortable: I regretted not bring my sponge sleeping mat. At some stage in the night I was woken up by the sound of a heavy vehicle crunching its way along the gravel road through the campsite. When I heard the crunching noise the second time, I realised it wasn't a vehicle: it was the sound of an avalanche sliding down the side of the mountains. Apparently this is normal in the Alps.

Day Two

We had planned to meet up with Patrick (the French guide) in the Le Praz Bar. Aran and I sat outside the café at a round table under an umbrella, watching the world pass us by: but wondering where the hell was Patrick? We were on our second coffee when Patrick arrived, fashionably late. It had been three years since we last saw him and he looked like he had just woken up; tassled salt n' pepper hair, unshaven, scruffily dressed, yawning continuously. Whilst making allowances for Patrick's state of tiredness he was approaching sixty and he was openly talking about retirement. It got worse: he then told us with some amusement that one eye was not working properly, to which Aran and I laughed nervously; this was the man who would guide us to safety across the Alps. Aran and Patrick babbled on in French for a long time, whilst Patrick chain-smoked roll ups. I was in non comprende zone, so I just sat and smiled like a simpleton. Occasionally Aran gave me a quick translation: "1 metre of snow on the mountain ridges and slopes means avalanche conditions, so the Monte Rosa is off the list". Then Patrick mentioned some other peaks that he was prepared to guide us across over the next five days. Patrick gulped down the last of his coffee, stubbed out his cigarette and started to inspect our rucksacks with some enthusiasm. He began to empty the contents of clothing and mountain gear piece by piece onto the café floor, spreading the gear right acros the café until the café resembled a jumble sale. If the item was good he nodded and gave a "hmm" sound, if the item was bad he shook his head and tutted. This was the kind of language that I understood. In summary: Aran's ruck sack was too big and my Ski coat was too thick. Alpine mountaineering was all about travelling light and fast, so big thick coats and big rucksacks were not required. Patrick seemed to enjoy this bit and insisted on us replacing the rejected equipment before we set off. Patrick's critical assessment was good news for our preparation - and even better news for the local retailers.

Day Three.

On a sun drenched morning, the three of us set off from Argentierre and arrived at the Telegraphic cable way which took us up the first stage of the mountain. We then ascended further by walking for three hours along well trodden paths that zig-zagged up to the Albert

Premier Hut. This hut had been built over a hundred years ago, next to the Glacier, long before the Premier Inn concept had been considered. The hut consisted of a communal dining area and communal sleeping areas to hold over one hundred people. After a hearty meal, we retired to our dormitory which slept twenty people, which was achieved by four rows of five adjacent beds. The unusual aspect of this hut was that before bedtime everybody took their mountaineering equipment into the crowded dormitory room with them instead of leaving it in the locker room near the entrance. The chaos materialised during the night when a frenchman came into the dorm and woke Aran up, insisting that Aran was sleeping in his bed. "Cest Moi!" he said, far too many times, and Aran vacated the spot to avoid causing a scene.

Day Four. Aguille De Tour

The snoring choir of twenty people started waking up at staggered intervals between 2.00 a.m. and 6.00 a.m. Each small waking group were shining torches around the dark room, rustling through plastic carier bags. When we woke at 5.30 a.m. the hut was almost empty. Why didn't they stay for breakfast? we asked: when we saw the breakfast of cold toast and coffee the answer became clear. We left the hut using our headtorches on a dark path that lead us to the rim of the glacier. As we stopped to put on our crampons and get roped up, I became aware of the dimly lit glacier lying before us. Now we were roped up, Patrick was in front, Aran in the middle and me at the back. It was great to walk with crampons on the snow and ice, crunching every step, knowing that you could not slip. We were roped up because the risk of falling down crevasses, and the idea was that the last person in the chain i.e. the one not falling down the crevasse would act as an anchor. It took a while to get used to being roped up and moving as a party of three; don't tread on the rope, don't let the rope go slack, keep it tight!

As Patrick guided us across the ice covered landscape opened up before us and all of the previous nights discomforts were quickly forgotten. It was like walking into the ice age. The spectacular scenary of the snow capped mountains of Chardonnay and Tete Blanche was impressive: and if that wasn't enough, Mont Blanc sat in the backdrop. We quickly turned west towards the "Letterbox" which was a gap between two rocks at the top of a ridge. Firstly, we had to march up a snow slope that gradually became steeper and steeper, to the extent where I considered that it was steep enough for front-pointing on the final approach. Patrick moved up the slope without breaking stride, and Aran was sure footed on the incline, despite his blisters. When we reached the top of the ridge we stopped for a break. Aran peeled off his socks.

"Somebody at the hut had taken my socks by mistake, so I borrowed a pair from the hut manager, but they are really thin. Look at these blisters…"

I nodded in sympathy. "Aran, what did your socks look like?"

"Black, thick, with a North Face logo," said Aran, who sounded depressed – he was very precious about his gear.

I looked around and Patrick was busy rolling up a cigarette, although his raised trousers revealed some black socks, with a North Face logo on - mitigating circumstances your honour – Patrick only had one eye.

We slowly got to our feet, and saw that beyond the letter box we could see the Col Du Tour open up before us. It was giant basin of snow at the foot of the surrounding mountains which emerged from the left and to the right. We turned left and went down the slope only to turn back up again towards to the Agulle de Tour. In the baking mid-morning sun we headed across a crevassed slope, stepping over the gap and then up a precarious scree slope which was a bit like walking through quick sand. Once that bit was done, we took off our crampons and spiralled our way up towards the rocky summit. Patrick had disappeared somewhere in front, but there wasn't much exposure and it was great fun bouldering up to the peak. Technically it was a basic scramble, like Bristly Ridge or Scafel, but less exposure. The peak gave us a great vantage point across the Col Du Tour to the west and the Mont Blanc range to the north. We spent a good fifteen minutes posing and posturing for photos amidst the alpine backdrop. We drank in the panoramic views as we eyed the other peaks with wonder about their accessibility. Hillwalking/mountaineering was like a drug, one peak was not enough and I was always looking for the next fix. We were surrounded by mountain peaks, and spoilt for choice. While we eyed up the other peaks like giddy kids Patrick was taking his next roll up 'fix' and sat down in the shade. He'd seen it all before.

When we reached the bottom, Patrick suddenly stopped and swore, he'd left some of his climbing equipment on the peak and he turned around to go back for it. Aran and I just sat in the mid-day sun on the slope and slowly baked in the mid day sun. We applied sun cream, but it was too late for that. The powerful sunlight reflected off the snow to create a dazzling brightness. In the early afternoon we felt relaxed and at peace with the world- apart from the sound of cracking glacier ice melting under the sun.

All we had to do now was cross the huge bowl of a glacier (Glacier de Tour and the Col de Tour) and reach the Trient hut, which we could see in the distance across the bowl. We roped up again and the three of us set off across the huge bowl which was fractured with cracks. Some of the cracks were a few inches wide and others were a few feet wide. The situation was complex as some of the latter were covered in deceptive "snow bridges". Patrick kept stopping to fathom out the location of the crevasses and the best route through it. We were glad to have a guide to navigate us through this minefield. As we crossed the French-Swiss border we could see the hut clearly in the distance, its Swiss flag fluttered in the breeze. It was with some relief when we reached the hut, sat down outside and slowly peeled off our gear, piece by piece, giving thankful groans after each item was discarded; coats, crampons, boots, socks, ahhh and then a glass of water; the simplest of luxuries in life. Then we limped around in our shorts, t-shirts and slippers looking for the most comfortable armchair inside the hut. After eight hours of adrenalin fuelled walking in the baking sun we had definitely earned our rest in this authentic mountain hut. After dinner, in the hut, the guides were all crowded around the radio listening to the Alpine weather forecast: not a word was spoken as everybody listened intently. All of the plans for mountain treks were reliant on decent weather. I couldn't understand a word of the French forecast, but it was just great to be there: open fire, books, maps and comfy sofas; Wainwright would have loved it here if only he would have actually visited the Alps. Patrick strutted around the hut with his new socks, whilst Aran limped around miserably due to blisters. As we melted into the armchairs, tiredness rapidly descended upon us and Aran confided that he might struggle to walk the next day - if they didn't heal up.

Unlike the last hut, the Trient had spacious dorms and they were half empty. For the first time ever, I managed to sleep properly in a mountain hut. This time I was out like a light, and most probably snoring for England.

Day Five (Tete Blanche)

At 5.15 a.m. I heard the door creak open, and Patrick half-whispered and half-shouted "Arraan, Arraaaan! It's 5.15!"

"Shit! I said, "we should have been meeting for breakfast at 5.00 a.m.!"

We scrambled around getting our gear together, and I went through the comedy routine of finding my camera-losing-my camera-and finding my camera again. Eventually I got my rucksack on and said "Ready!" and looked round to find that Aran and Patrick were gone.

They were waiting outside in the dark. We switched on our head torches and set off across the path that lead straight down to the cracked and fractured Glacier de Tour.

The three of us, roped up, set off at a fast pace into the darkness of the crevasse minefield. It was the same glacier that we traversed across the day before. This time we walked without crampons so our feet felt lighter, enjoying the sound and sensation of crunching a thin layer of snow beneath the feet. As we moved quickly across the glacier this time, the snow and ice was hard underfoot (unlike yesterday afternoon) and therefore the crevasses were smaller and easier to cross. In the darkness there was less fear of the crevasses. After all what you can't see can't hurt you, right? The snow itself provided some white light of its own which slowly began to gather strength. We headed towards the French Alps approaching the Tete Blanche at the end of the basin. Patrick began to zig-zag his way as we got closer to the Tete Blanche. We blasted across the Glacier Du Col, making good time, fully warmed up and enjoying the adrenalin fuelled traverse across firm snow under foot. Slowly, we became aware of the first signs of the sun waking up, and an evolving sunset: creating an everchanging spectrum of colours as the sunlight from the east reflected off the Italian and Swiss Alps. It was a tapestry of colours that can only be created by nature itself: it was impossible to capture the full beauty of this magnificent scene with a camera, but that didn't stop us trying.

The dreamlike ambience of the sunset was rudely awakened by a stark reality in front of us. We noticed a huge crevasse fifteen feet wide (and God knows how deep deep) running from the foot of the Tete Blanche right the way along the glacier, blocking our way entirely to the Tete Blanche. Patrick was heading towards a snow bridge that went over the crevasse to the foot of the Tete Blanche Mountain. It seemed like the only sensible option.

We inched forwards and stopped our crunching march as Patrick pondered on the next move, and we stood listening to the near silence. "Spread out, this is dangerous, in case one of us falls into the crevasse, we need to pull each other out. Keep the rope tight."

Now that we stopped walking and talking, I became aware of a stillness in the air. Only the slightest breeze could be heard, although my heartbeat seemed almost audible as I looked down into the gaping jaws of the crevasse before us. "Difficult to guess how deep this crevasse is," I said. "But I'd rather not know."

Patrick told us to get our crampons on as he lengthened the rope so he was about forty feet in front of us as he tentatively approached the snow bridge, which sloped upwards. Patrick said something in French to Aran and Aran leaned back keeping the rope tight; so I did the same, getting a firm foothold in the snow. I was the last in line, so I was the last anchor point if the other two fell into the black hole. It was a grim thought and I wondered if this "snow bridge" option was normal. Patrick set off across the abyss. He spread eagled himself to even out his body weight as he crawled forwards across the bridge. At one point, in the middle he stopped and looked down into the crevasse and shouted "it's as deep as a house!" Once he finally crossed we breathed a sigh of relief and Aran began to cross over the bridge, and I noticed that due to the angle of the slope he slipped slighty as he was spread eagled. He crossed over safely and now it was my turn. For some reason when I got half way across I started to kick in some steps to prevent sliding off the bridge.

"What are you doing?" shouted Patrick, after muttering something in French.

Aran translated into Anglo Saxon "Gaz, stop kicking you'll bring the bridge down!"

"Okay, okay," I said as I crossed safely to other side.

With that obstacle cleared we had the small matter of climbing the mountain. The three of us stood looking up at the Tete Blanche as Patrick marched off towards the first rocky boulders at the base. Crampons off, we started to scramble using our hands on the rock as there wasn't much snow on the east part of the mountain. There is something very natural about bare hands on rocks, especially when the rocks have been warmed by the early morning sun. It felt safer on rock than on snow and ice. White stuff kills – I think I've already mentioned that earlier.

Patrick started use his spider like frame to full effect across the simple rock scramble and occasionally disappeared from view. There were two memorable parts to this scramble. Firstly a ledge; it was around 2 metres long and around six inches wide with a 10 metre drop below to the left and a flat smooth rock to the right - and you guessed it, the rock face on the right did not have any handholds. Patrick skipped acros the ledge so quickly that I didn't have time to observe his technique. Then it was Aran's turn as he moved across steadily pressing his body into the rock face as he shuffled crab like across the ledge. Next it was my turn, and I couldn't make my mind up; skip across it like Patrick or spiderman style like Aran. In the end I opted for the latter as I half heartedly shuffled across, like a drunken crab.

"Move your body into the rock," said Aran as I leaned my body a bit closer to the rock in an awkward smooch dance. It was awkward because I had my arse sticking out, as I wanted to watch my feet. After that episode we did some straightforward scrambling around the route which spiralled around the mountain to the summit. Aran was looping the rope around rocky boulders on some sections, which seemed reassuring, as Patrick was way up ahead and we never knew if he was putting in any protection slings for us higher up. "Has Patrick put any protection in up there?" was my repetitive question, and to be fair Aran didn't know either. The north face was steeper and most of the rocks were covered in snow. Below us there was a steep drop, which Aran admired greatly; but my admiration was less vocal and I preferred to look up as Aran looped the rope around a rock and raced up the slope kicking in snow steps, generally looking like he knew what he was doing, while I held onto the rope in a striding position, as instructed.

"Okay, ready!" Aran shouted down to me, and I set off up the 4 metre steep slope kicking in steps as I went. It soon became apparent that there were no hand holds, so I began to claw at the snow steps above my head. "Don't touch the snow with your bare hands! They will be useless once they are frozen," said Aran. It made sense but I genuinely did not know what else to do with my hands, so I guess I ignored his advice and carried on. My actions were due to the fact that I was used to unroped scrambling where the four point contact rule applies and reducing this to two points was frowned upon. Now I was in a different world of roped scrambling up snow and ice slopes - so different rules apply, I guess: I say "I guess" because I don't know how to scramble without hands.

Anyway, without further ado we reached the broad summit of Tete Blanche, in a hot and sweaty state that accompanies many climaxes in life. Coats and hats were removed to cool down in the afterglow. We stood up on the summit slab which seemed to be the highest point on this table top summit. The views were tremendous. We looked round and saw Patrick sitting in between two rocks that formed a makeshift armchair, rolling up another cigarrette, looking bored. After all, he had seen this all before.

Meanwhile, Aran and I were buzzing and started to enjoy the fantastic views all around us. To our south at the foot of the mountain was the gaping hole of the huge crevasse running east to west that we had crossed. In the backdrop the vast Glacier de Tour and Swiss Trient hut that we had set off from this morning was a tiny speck in the distance. We clicked away with our cameras, focussing on the snow bridge that had survived the kicking. To our north lay the Aguille De Tour which we had climbed yesterday, which seemed like a long time ago now. To the south we could see the picture postcard ridge of Chardonnay. As we exhausted the number photograph angles that could possibly be taken, the excitement and adrenalin slowed down as we took our seats on the rock slabs, not far from Patrick's armchair. It's difficult to underestimate the melting pot of physical and mental emotions when sitting on top of an alpine summit; the exertion, relief, pride, glowing satisfaction - and the desperate need to go for a pee.

Patrick's character was unravelling as the days went by. There wasn't much small talk, just instructions on what was needed, especially on crevassed areas. His small scruffy appearance was deceptive. His speed of movement across the glaciers and the rocky scrambles was very impressive. His clothes were light, and he never stopped to take stuff in and out of his rucksack such as gloves, hats, extra layers of clothes, axes, food, drink. Everything seemed to be clipped to his belt. Patrick's rucksack was small and looked half empty. He carried rope looped around his shoulder: it seemed he had the bare essentials, and nothing more. His methodology was completely compatible with Alpine climbing; fast and continuous movement and light equipment. The concept worked in this environment - getting the climbs/walks done as early as possible before the peaks became busy and before the longer hours of sun could start to change the condition of the snow and ice into less reliable conditions; softer snow, melting ice, more rockfalls and bigger crevasses. Aran and I were also becoming aware that Patrick didn't really seem to eat or drink much, and when we offered him food he nearly always refused it. This seemed strange due the amount of energy required to cover physical distance and terrain we were covering. All of this added to the mysterious portfolio – God knows what he thought of us.

As we slowly descended the Tete Blanche roped up together, Aran and myself were babbling away in excitement, pointing at nearby peaks and asking Patrick if we could do another peak.

There was no doubt about it, we were on a mental and physical high, and were becoming mountaineering junkies. Wait a minute, I was a hill walker before. Am I a mountaineer now? At the time, I probably thought so despite my inability to understand the basic rope knots, or develop a confident crampon technique on steep snow slopes. As we rapidly descended the south side of TB, we continued to take photographs one handed and chatter away, intoxicated with mountain fever. Once we reached the bottom the enjoyment of walking down the gradual descending snow slopes continued. Every now and then we skipped over a crevasse and Patrick became serious again. "No photos now" and "Keep the ropes tight" and then the impossibile request "No talking!" We entered into the gap between Chardonnay and Tete Blanche heading in the direction of the Albert Premier Hut.

Although Aran and myself were in happy clappy "la, la land" at this stage, we only realised when we returned home that our friend Andy had confirmed that twenty years earlier two of his friends from Leeds Polytechnic had descended from Chardonnay and fallen down a crevasse on the same area that Aran and I had crossed. The haunting aspect was that one of the unlucky climbers had survived for two days afterwards at the bottom of the crevasse awaiting rescue to no avail.

We saw a group of German mountaineers approach Patrick and their leader asked him for directions to the Letterbox (the short cut to the Swiss border). Patrick continued walking and barked back at him "Look at your map! Or if you can't read a map, go down to Chamonix and hire yourself a guide!"

We wanted to tell the Germans they already walked straight past it. "No, say nothing," said Patrick. "There are unemployed guides in Chamonix and these arrogant guys just want it all for free."

Aran and I said nothing. Patrick's conscience got the better of him, as five minutes later he shouted to the five Germans in french and pointed them in the direction of the letterbox. The five of them formed a conference circle around a map, debating the authenticity of Patrick's advice. I was so glad we had hired a guide. It was worth every Euro.

With world peace restored, we crossed another three crevasses to start our way across the Glacier De Tour, this time without crampons and in the daylight. We could now see a winter wonderland of strange ice formations: darker smoother ice underfoot littered with the occasional crevasse. Once we passed the Albert Hut we could see the clouds moving in, and by the time we had taken the telepherique (cableway) down to Argentierre at 2 p.m. we felt the first spots of rain. Tired, and jubilant we ordered some cool beers in the pizza bar at Argentierre. As we watched the rain trickle down the pub window we decided to abandon the idea of camping out and booked into a local guesthouse: we'd earned it.

We celebrated with some more beers and started to talk about Mont Blanc - after all we were hardened mountaineers now. By late evening our confidence was brimming like the froth of the beers spilling over our fifth drink.

"Hey Aran, do you reckon we could do Mont Blanc via the Three Monts route?"

"Yeah, why not? We will ask Patrick tomorrow" said Aran as he wiped the froth from his upper lip.

DAY FOUR – Argentierre.

As predicted, today was a complete washout. Not only did It rain all day but it was heavy rain with thunder and lightning. It was a perfect day to recover from the previous three days' exertions on the mountains. In Argentierre, at the foot of the steep valley, it was the best place to be as we could properly nurse our hangover and our sore feet.

The alternative option of going up on the peaks was not good. Above 2,500 metres was entertaining heavy snow, low cloud and lightning.

DAY SIX – Aiguille De Toule (3534m)

Patrick picked us up in Argentierre and drove us to Courmayeur (the Italian side of the Alps) via the Mont Blanc tunnel. It was the nearest we got to Mont Blanc. Although we had never climbed Mont Blanc, at least we could now claim to have gone under it. Courmayear was baked in sun at 10.00 a.m. and Patrick instructed us that in order to get a discount on the Telepherique up to the Torina Hut, Aran and I should pretend to be mountain guides (it brought the price down to 76 Euros in total for the three of us). When we stepped off the cable car and walked into the Torina hut it appeared to be old, clean and authentic. There were three reasons that this was a great mountain hut: The hut is perched high near the mountain peaks. On the South side was Mont Blanc and adjacent to the Don de Geant; hospitable and friendly. The Italians are great hosts. They actually ask you what route you are climbing and your expected return; Reasonable prices for food and drinks (and a decent bar).

The hut was brilliantly located in the centre of some of the most impressive peaks in the Alps. The hut seemed to attract purely climbing clientele with no evidence of tourists. This made sense as there were no gentle walks across the valley blanche. It seemed that Aran and myself were now rubbing shoulders with real alpine climbers. I felt that I had been promoted from 'hill walker' to 'mountaineer' all in the same vacation - but in reality it felt that we were both 'on trial'.

Not long after reaching the Torino hut we left as much gear as possible in the hut and stepped out straight into the Glacier du Geant. We moved quickly to keep up with Patrick who was setting the pace; our rucksacks were light and we wore thin coats. The Dent Du Geant was immediately to our right; a tooth shaped mountain which pointed up to the sky. It dominated the nearby landscape. We could see several climbers making their way up the Dent De Geant, and it looked like a vertical climb from where we were.

After the three of us roped up, we strode across the snow, and once again it was great to feel the snow crunch beneath our feet. It was already late morning and the sun blazed down directly above us. The snow was becoming soft beneath our feet. The Glacier du Geant was quite busy as cable cars hummed just a few metres above our heads going in a straight line past the Torino hut in the direction of the Aguille de Midi. Bizarrely, the cable car could be taken from the Italian alps to the French alps at a distance of around ten miles. They seemed like a surreal addition to the stunning glaciers and superb alpine scenary: the passengers were uninvited guests from another age. On the ground, people were heading back to the Torino hut in drips and drabs. It felt quite late to be setting off on our latest expedition to a peak called Aiguille De Toule, which was another mountain we had never heard of. Although it sounded very much like the peak that we did three or four days ago. Aguille De Tour? Perhaps Patrick was making all of this up as he went along?

One man staggered towards us, walking rather unsteadily. As he passed us by I noticed his face was red and swollen.

Aran turned around and said "Altitude sickness." I nodded sympathetically remembering the Gran Paradiso. It was a reminder of where we were. Another reminder was our approach to a sizable crevasse that we crossed over with caution. Patrick looked around at both of us, and the tone of his voice was serious.

"Stop talking. No photos now."

We crossed over another two crevasses before we turned left down the Vallee Blanche, as we heard the cracking noise of rocks falling down the mountain onto the glacier. The echo of the falling rocks was unnerving, especially as some smaller pieces rolled down into the snow based valley where we were walking.

The Vallee Blanche was basically a giant bath tub full of ice, with steep sided mountains on either side. As we walked in the direction of the Three Monts, we were surrounded by mountain peaks and I began to wonder which one was the Aguille De Toule. Patrick turned sharply to the south and we started to ascend a snow slope that became steeper and steeper. As we ascended it became a real physical challenge and I started to breathe more heavily. However, my main concern was that the higher we went, the thinner the surface snow became, which meant that my feet were no longer making the gripped footprints in the snow. We took a diagonal line to take more side steps up the mountain. Another concern was that the 5mm of snow that our crampon blades were clinging to was 5mm of soft melting snow.

"Hey Aran, the snow is in poor condition," I said, trying to sound like a professional mountaineer, as my feet began to slip a little on each step.

"I know. The midday sun is baking the slopes," said Aran as he continued to make delicate but confident steps up the mountain.

I continued along the diagonal line going up the slope. How steep was it? Forty degree angle? Who knows. All I knew was that my ankles were aching with leaning into the slope, and my calfs were singing a painful ballad. Patrick had now slowed down to a stop as he surveyed the slope above us, trying to choose the best line to the summit. Aran looked down the slope, and I did the same to notice how far up the mountain we had traversed. I instantly regretted the decision to look down: at the bottom of the Vallee Blanche I could see climbers the size of ants walking in their groups of roped up ants. The fear of heights registered in my brain, transferring to the butterflies in the stomache and then it got worse - the legs began to wobble ever so slightly. I also became aware that if one of us slipped then the three of us would be pulled down down this mountain in a rapid tangle of sharp crampons, rope and ice axes.

"Aran, is Patrick going to put in some protection? An ice screw or something?"

"I don't know, I'll ask him," said Aran.

I looked up to see the rocky summit of the Aiguille De Toule above us, with around 100 metres of this forty-five degrees of slushy ice slope lying between us. I guessed that Patrick and Aran had the same concerns as me, as we remained stationary for a long time while Patrick decided on the next move. A silence descended on the slope. Nobody said anything. I had a grip on the snow, but I had been stood in the same position, balancing my weight with my left foot behind, which was supported by my walking pole that I using as additional support, and then my right foot was in front pointing up the slope. I also had an axe in my right hand, which I gripped intensely knowing that the axe was my only real anchor in the event of a slip. My calfs were screaming with pain at this point, and I tried to take my mind off the situation to lessen the pain. The waiting seemed to take an age as we stood waiting for Patrick to make the next move.

Aran seemed a bit more relaxed about the situation, and gave me words of reassurance. It seemed to me that using the walking stick and axe combination gave the best of both worlds; the stick for balance and stability and the axe for a anchor. I'm not sure if this combination complies with text book mountaineering, but it seemed to help me.

Patrick was looking down the slope at us and shouted.

"Gary, put the stick away in your rucksack. You only need your axe." The angle of the slope was so steep that I couldn't lean backwards to slot my walking stick back into the rucksack, as I was leaning forwards into the slope, clinging on for dear life. Why couldn't he give this instruction earlier when we weren't in a such a precarious position? Also, I could not take my rucksack off without using two hands, and I needed my hands for the axe anchor in case of a slip. I was regretting not doing any crampon training on this second visit to the Alps.

"Aran, tell him in French that I might slip if I put my stick away. I'm going to use my stick and axe." It was a catch 22 situation.

Aran communicated my complaint up to Patrick. I don't know what Patrick said, and that was probably a good thing. Patrick grumbled something and started to walk around inspecting the slushy ice, and finally took out an ice screw and fixed it into the ice, with his rope connected. Finally we had some protection against a slip. Our hopes and dreams were resting on this ice screw firmly placed into a flavourless slush puppy.

We finally continued up the slope, which continued to get steeper: it was a relief to move again, even though the condition of the snow and ice was terrible. It was becoming more difficult to perform angled steps on this gradient and Aran started to use the front pointing technique on the final 10 metre stretch of the slope, which was basically leaning forwards close to the ice, using only the crampon spikes on your toes, and stepping up the slope using your axe infront as an anchor. He covered the ground nicely and now it was my turn: I began putting two hands on my axe, fixing it into the ice and then stepping upwards using the front toes. It was a bit like going up the stairs on your stomach, except the drop was several hundred metres and one slip would result in a broken leg - or maybe more. Strangely enough I felt more comfortable getting into the rhythm of doing this than standing still for ten minutes on the slushy ice slope. A few more exhausting steps and I'd made it onto the rock where Aran was waiting on the rocky ridge.

"Thank God for that." I said still panting from the last stretch. We congratulated each other, and I was just hoping that we wouldn't descend on the same route. We looked up towards the summit, but there was no sign of Patrick, or any protection. He was somewhere in front. It was difficult to get used to the "silent trust" involved in Alpine climbing. It seemed to be all about minimal communication and moving quickly.

We scrambled over the granite rocks, and once again it felt good to touch the warm rocks with bare hands. There was some exposure on the ridge, but not quite as much as a scramble across Striding Edge or Sharp Edge. As we reached the end of the ridge we saw Patrick sitting down rolling up a cigarette: this was clear sign that we had reached the summit. We immediately took off our rucksacks and admired the breathtaking views all around us: Dent Du Geant to the east, Aguille Du Midi to the north and Mont Tacul, Mont Maudit and Mont Blanc to the west. Nearby to the west was the Entreve and the Du Ronde and to the south the Gran Paradiso. We were the only people on the peak, but our location seemed to be perfectly central to many other peaks: effectively we were surrounded by peaks roughly the same height that we were at. Aran and I keep looking around the 360 degree panaromic view, mesmerised in disbelief that such Alpine scenary was attainable. I stood up doing a 360 degree video and lost my footing and stumbled. I swore, and reminded myself of the sheer drop just a few feet to the south down to Courmayeur.

"Shit, I nearly fell down there," I said, pointing down to Courmeyer.

"The mountain gives and the mountain takes!" said Aran drily.

We laughed and tucked into our snack of spicy sausage and cheese. A great combination of fat and protein (it was becoming our expedition diet). It tasted good and even Patrck accepted some and sliced off a piece of sausage with his knife. Once we had finished with all of the camera footage we relaxed and just took in the views with a quiet appreciation - it was a six course meal to feast your eyes on. There was a spooky quietness on the peak as if we should not have been there: we had gatecrashed a party, without a special invitation from the mountain Gods to access the summit. On closer inspection of life below, we could see ant like clusters of climbers at the base of the Vallee Blanche in their daisy chain formations. We could also see some small dots of people climbing Mont Tacul. The kind weather was to be savoured as we enjoyed the bright sun and the beautiful blue sky: the only thing that moved was the conveyer belt of fluffy white clouds that drifted over our heads. At our eye level the other peaks stood proudly, but they seemed accessible and inviting. Another peak often resulted in an urge to climb a slightly more challenging peak; mountain climbing was addictive – and now I could see why. Below us the snow capped glacier of the Vallee Blanche. Humans were now only just visible, like small dots. It was a truly humbling experience to be in this beautiful place. I could go on a bit more, but I am sure you get the picture.

Patrick stubbed out his cigarette, stood up and started to put his rucksack on, it was a signal that it was time to leave the summit and we reluctantly left the Aguille De Toule via the other side of the mountain. It was not quite as steep as our access route. All three of us, roped up again with walking sticks fully extended began our descent slowly and carefully. Patrick was kicking in steps with his heel and Aran followed by kicking in a bit more, so when I reached Aran's footprint the steps were already there. The first part was quite steep: we were all quiet, knowing that most slips on mountain climbs were on the descent when people were more tired, complacent and not focussing. After this first part, the rest of the descent was surprisingly easy. I couldn't take my eyes off the views below us. As we continued downwards we passed a group of climbers ascending labouriously. They looked exhausted. I noticed their red contorted faces, puffing and panting and wondered if we had looked like this during our ascent, but this feeling of wonder was overshadowed with the smug satisfaction knowing that our hard work was mainly done.

This part of the hike was so enjoyable. When we reached the lower slopes any thoughts of mountaineering hardship eased away. We followed the hypnotic rhythm of downward steps into soft snow. Leaning the body weight on the heel was so much easier than leaning on the front foot.

Meanwhile on the sun baked lower slopes, the snow was getting softer and we began to slide down ski-style until we reached the bottom of the Vallee Blanche. Then we had that serious business of crossing over many crevasses. As we got nearer to the Torino hut with the cable cars above us, we admired the majestic Dent Du Geant to our left. It was at this point around 3 p.m. that we heard a crackling noise coming from the rocks – it sounded like distant gun shots.

"Aran, what's that noise?" I said.

"Rockfall," said Aran, as the noise of falling rocks echoed through the valley, became increasingly loud. Strangely enough although the noise was coming from the rocky cliffs nearby to our right, I couldn't see the falling rocks. My eyes were fixed to the right, with occasional glances to the ground.

"There!" Aran pointed to several big boulders bouncing down the cliff making a terrific noise, taking smaller fragments with them. The rock debris thudded into the snowy ground at the bottom of the cliff, and one football sized boulder made a dull thud as it landed about 30 metres to our right, partially buried. The glacial mountain range seemed to be falling apart. At the Torino hut we sat on the west facing porch slowly taking our boots off, and stretched our wet clothes on the balcony area to dry them out. There were a couple of guys (from the same guest house as us) who were telling us about their adventure climbing the Dent Du Geant. As we listened we stared at the west face of the Mont Blanc in the distance; surely one day we would climb it in better conditions - but not the west side which looked like an impossible route. Then I became acutely aware of a low rumbling noise, and it sounded like a distant plane getting closer.

"Avalanche," said Aran

"No, it's a plane," I said, unconvincingly.

The noise grew louder and we could then see a giant ball of white cloud rolling down the west face of Mont Blanc.

Aran turned to ask one of the other climbers. "What would you do if you were under that cloud of snow?"

"I would say Ffffffffuuuuuu… and that's probably about all I could do."

With enough excitement for one day, we sat down and had our evening meal with the other climbers on the communal table who began telling stories of mountain climbs. Aran and I listened intently, hoping they wouldn't expect an epic story in return - our mountaineering CVs were quite thin.

Patrick stayed quiet and smiled cynically. When the story tellers had left the table, Patrick leaned over the table towards Aran and I, and said "Bullshit! I've never heard such bullshit, most of these guys…" he lifted up his hands to the Gods.

Aran and myself laughed heartily: this was just what the doctor ordered - pure entertainment. I noticed that Patrick wasn't really eating much food, so I made a point.

"Patrick, are you not hungry?"

"No," said Patrick, and rubbed his stomach with a pained expression and went off to bed.

Aran and myself went to the bar and ordered some beer to see if we could do some damage to our stomaches. The bar was busy but not overcrowded as the whole room was decked out in comfy olde worlde sofas, tables with old maps, maps on the walls, photographs of an SAS training course from 2002 - it was like a climbing museum. Next came two younger guys who sat down opposite us and began to ask us questions about climbing, peaks and weather conditions. Aran and I just told them of our recent adventures and they sat on the edge of their chairs eagerly and they must have thought we were experienced mountaineers, when in reality we were just older and could weave a better story together without blinking too much. As more characters of all nationalities drifted into the bar, the old fashioned heaters began to make me drowsy: the adrenalin from the day had now been replaced with tiredness. It had been another great day in Alpine paradise.

DAY SEVEN - AIGUILLE DE ENTREVES (3600m)

At around 5.00 a.m. Aran's jolly-but-weird alarm woke me up. Aran stirred, Patrick coughed and then it seemed that everyone drifted off again. At 5.30 a.m. the now familiar and less weird alarm went off again and we trudged off to the dining hall for a grim early morning breakfast. Most people had already eaten and set off for the mountains. Patrick didn't eat anything and he just shuffled back towards the dormitory looking ill. We ate our breakfasts in near silence and I met up with Aran in the kit room. We started to get our gear ready. It was a slick routine now: boots on, not too many layers of clothes, helmets and head torches on. After three separate mountain days we knew which stuff to leave behind in the plastic trays in the hut. There was still no sign of Patrick as put our helmets on. I noticed that Aran's movements were also slow.

"Are you tired?" I said.

"Yeah, I'm knackered."

"Each day is physically tougher than the previous day – which is okay - but technically it's also getting tougher each day. I'm getting out of my depth. I'm a walker at heart, not much climbing on my CV…"

Aran nodded as he adjusted his straps on his helmet.

"No sign of Patrick?" I said.

"I think he's gone back to bed."

"Maybe we get a day off?" I said, half hoping that we would cancel the next mountain trip and do something easy.

Suddenly, the small waif like figure of Patrick emerged from shadows, fully kitted out carrying his crampons in his hands.

"Allez," grunted Patrick as he lead the way out of the Torino hut, and within a few minutes we were trudging through the snow of the Vallee Blanche. The cold breeze woke me up instantly, and the rising sun had illuminated that spectacular mountain scenery that we couldn't take our eyes off. Dent du Geant was on our right as we turned left and headed towards the Three Monts. It was becoming like a morning commute.

"Du Ronde is out of condition, so today we will do the Aiguille d' Entreves," said Patrick, who seemed a bit perkier now.

It made no difference to Aran or me – it was another mountain that we had never heard of. Will it be tougher than yesterday I thought?

I noticed that a group of Italian soldiers were climbing the same mountain that we climbed yesterday, but notably they were on a different ascent route that was less steep.

We skipped over crevasses now without breaking stride, making casual comments about the width and depth. Three days ago it would have raised the pulse rate.

Patrick swiftly turned towards the Entreve, and I was a bit anxious about the steepness of the snow slope. To my pleasant surprise the direct route taken went through a nice depth of six inch snow which was in okay condition. On the ascent we focussed on footwork and camera shots whilst Patrick wasn't looking. He turned round to Aran.

"Rope tight!"

At last up on the top, we rested on the corniced snowy ridge, with the rocky ridge of the Entreve to our right. I couldn't see the peak, partially obscured by a rocky ridge, but was nice to take off the crampons and scramble across the warm rocks.

The ridge went up and down like a rollercoaster and became narrower. I began to feel at home, despite the loose slabs. This was fun scrambling, and Patrick moved like a spider across the rocks. Occasionally we would look down the Courmayeur to the left, a sheer drop that made my stomach do somersaults. All this fun came to a stop when the ridge ran all the way up a narrow pilar shaped summit, and beyond that was a sea of blue sky. It was going to be a white knuckle ride of a scramble to the summit. Suddenly, Patrick moved off the crest and headed down to a lower steeper section, and we dutifully followed, becoming aware of sheer drops to the right down the Vallee Blanche. As we skirted around the rock face with some four point scrambling I could see that Patrick was aiming for the steepest ascent to the summit: a 40 metre steeple like tower.

"Jesus Christ, it's a near vertical rock face! Can't we go up along the crested ridge?" I said. But I seemed to speaking a different language as Patrick started getting himself ready for the rock climb. I had never rock climbed in my life before, apart from a climbing wall at *Centre Parcs*. Now, at the age of forty-two, it seemed a bit late to start.

"Are we going up to the summit that way?" I said, pointing at the 40 metre vertical rock face.

"Yes, you'll be okay" said Patrick, smiling.

As Patrick began to lead the climb, scuttling upwards, I then turned to Aran for a bucket load of sympathy.

"Aran, I'm out of my depth here." I was trying to hide the panic in my voice.

"Patrick's the guide. He must think we are capable of doing this."

"You know, the crest of the ridge looks like a better option," I said, but nobody was listening. Protest was futile - the guide called the shots and we just followed. There's no democracy in climbing. I tried to concentrate on which handholds Patrick was using, but he was climbing so fast, it was a bit a blur.

Patrick kept a disciplined body shape and moved with agility. He was clearly enjoying himself and soon he reached the top. Although we could not see him, we heard a shout. Aran wasn't ruffled in the slightest as he had done some rock climbing in his student days with Andy in Scotland and the Alps. Now, I wished I had joined them on their weekend climbing trips instead of concentrating on cigarettes and alcohol consumption.

It was Aran's turn next, and the rope tightened. I watched his moves intently. There was a verticle crack that ranged from six inches to three inches, and Aran remained faithful to the crack for handholds and footholds. I also noticed that Aran used his feet well and seemed to put most of his weight onto his feet. He scaled up the flat sided rock face with confidence, and as soon as he finished to pitch and reached the top, he shouted down.

"Okay Gaz!"

I looked up at the cathedral like steeple going up to the sky, and then below me into the plummeting depths of the Vallee Blanche: there was no question of turning back.

"Okay, I'm climbing, watch me now!" I said, trying to sound confident.

I took in a deep breath and the first few steps seemed easy with some jugholds and decent footholds a plenty. The steeper the rock face became the smoother the rocks and the climb gradually demanded technical skills; finding the best handholds and footholds was creative art. I tried to increase my speed and get into a rhythm like Aran did, but I struggled to find the footholds. My thick soled, unbendable boots were crampon friendly but not thin enough to manouvre into tiny cracks. Despite the lack of experience, I seemed to muddle through the climb. I knew that I had rope protection, although It did not feel natural to rely on the tightness of the rope. Amidst some kind of embarrassingly emotional relief I eventually

reached the top of the Entreve summit. I was glowing with pride.

"I was shitting myself!" I said to Patrick, who laughed like a child, clearly enjoying the

spectacle as he brought up the rope and looped it around boulders. Patrick clearly understood

my limits and he just smiled as he started to roll up his cigarette. Patrick and Aran were

sitting uncomfortably close together, half sitting half standing. Once I got my breath back and

had finished shaking, I stepped up I realised that the summit was the size of a postage stamp,

and we were forming some kind of awkward pyramid. Once I stood up, I understood the

reason why Patrick and Aran were perched in strange positions - because the summit was not

wide enough to comfortably accommodate three people. Aran, who seemed to be completely

immune to vertigo, tried to stand up to get a higher perspective, but Patrick immediately told

him to sit down.

Aran took lots of photographs, and I took some shaky snaps from my fixed position. It was

like peering out of an eagles nest, and the feeling of exposure was immense. I must confess I

didn't look down too much, because I was trying to take my mind off climbing down. Just

when I started to relax Patrick stubbed out his cigarette.

"Okay Gary, you go down first," said Patrick. "Just slide down on your arse,"

This guy is having a laugh I thought, surely the golden rule is never to scramble down with

your back to the rock face? I was perplexed and looked at Aran - but resistance to a guide's

instruction is futile. I was slow learner.

So I decided to ignore Patrick, and climb down facing the rock.

"No, turn round with your back to the rock, we have a tight rope," said Patrick.

He was really serious about this. I turned round briefly but couldn't see what I was doing, so I

faced the rock again, using handholds and footholds to take the pressure off the rope. As I got

nearer to the bottom of the steeple tower I started to... enjoy myself. The feeling of relief was overwhelming when I reached the bottom of the pillar, and I wondered if there was a potential enjoyment that could be extracted from this rock climbing business. As I stood in the belay position, I shouted up.

"Okay, ready."

When Aran and Patrick had reached the bottom of the pillar we moved back across the crested ridge. The ridge seemed like child's play compared to the rock climb we had just done. At the lower flatter section of the rocks, near the snow line we sat down in more spacious surrounding this time and started to tuck into our staple diet of sausage, cheese, nuts, raisins and water. I looked down into the Vallee Blanche straining to see the ant-sized climbers far below, but none could be seen. They had all been absorbed into the Alpine landscape.

We made our way back down the snow slopes into the valley. The Entreve was the last peak of the tour, and it was by far the most technically challenging. It was good to eventually get down into the valley, knowing that we had completed our final mountain climb of the tour. The four peaks we had completed in recent days were both physically and mentally draining, but the adrenalin was still pumping and I was tingling with excitement. There was so much drama here in the Vallee Blanche with mountains all around this basin. And let's face it – it seemed like the glacier was falling apart: rockfalls, avalanches and crevasses were in abundance, and that was before you started to climb the mountains.

I cannot understate the enjoyment of the camaraderie of walking across the snow, ice and rock with Patrick and Aran in the magnificent Alpine wonderland. Essentially, we were moving together as a team, although we had no choice as we were roped up. We had been moving in unison across the glaciers and mountains, even though I didn't know where we were going or what we were doing for half of the time. I've no apologies for repeating this but being outdoors in the snow under the warm sun was good for the soul, a million miles away from the stresses and strains of working long hours back home. There was also a soulful simplicity of the mountaineering life: walk, climb, eat, sleep and the same again the next day. There was nothing much to think about, apart from concentrating on where we were putting our feet. As we crossed the Col de Blanche towards the hut we saw a guide training some novices how to climb out of a crevasse. Patrick smiled as we walked past the training session. He stopped and turned around to speak to Aran and myself.

"They will forget everything as soon as they get their crampons on." We laughed heartedly. After all, we were experienced mountaineers now.

"Hey Patrick, shouldn't we be learning these techniques of getting out of crevasses?" I said.

"Ah, you will soon learn to pull the rope when your friend disappears down a crevasse in front of you, and you try to pull him out!".

We all laughed again, but Aran and myself did not laugh as loudly as Patrick.

"What about Mont Blanc?" I said to Patrick.

"The snow is out of condition, heavy snow and mild conditions are perfect for avalanches," said Patrick.

Aran and myself shrugged, happy to take the sensible guidance.

"There are some guides, desperate for money who will take you. It's a gamble. Some guides die young. Not me though, I'm sixty."

"There are *bold* mountaineers and *old* mountaineers, but never both," said Aran, repeating the well-coined phrase. We both laughed, and Aran explained the joke in French and Patrick smiled and nodded, but he didn't laugh: for him I can only guess that there were probably some ghosts scattered around the Alps.

JEBEL SHAMS - APRIL 2012

In the middle of the night, somewhere in the emptiness of the Arabian desert a small convoy of three cars headed towards the Hajar Mountains in Oman. Our plan was to travel from Dubai to Oman and hike up to the highest peak in Oman, Jebel Shams (*the mountain of the sun*) over the weekend. Geoff, Derek, Roy, Talal, Ihab and me had planned the trip several weeks in advance. To be honest Geoff had done most of the planning and the rest of us followed in the slipstream. Our group of walkers possessed a good sense of adventure and varying degrees of fitness. We had met up at 1.00 a.m. on a Friday morning on the outskirts of Dubai, at the Dubai Retail Park. The population of Dubai (like the rest of the Gulf) clung to the coastline, and once you travelled 5 miles inland you had arrived in the vastness of the desert.

The headlights of the Mitsibishi Pajero lit up the empty road in front of us. Tonight we were the only people travelling across the desert. There were two thoughts entering my mind: either the privileged six of us knew that night travel was necessary to open the door to mountain adventure or we were idiots and we could have been lying in bed with our wives (individually and not collectively, of course).

All those doubts disappeared when the first hints of sunrise began to slowly unveil the gentle rolling landscape of the desert. The dim light began to slowly replace the complete darkness and gradually the occasional sand dune, sparse vegetation and herds of camels roaming across the beautiful desert plains became visible. The United Arab Emirates consisted of seven emirates: Abu Dhabi (home of the oil money), Dubai (home of alcohol) Sharjah (home of islamic culture and no alcohol), Arjman (which had alcohol), Furjairah (beautiful deserts, rural hills and villages) Umm-al- Qain (a mixture of the above) and Ras-Al-Khaimah (home of spectacular mountains, including the *stairway to Heaven*).

The UAE conjures up images of its excessive wealth and materialism, when in fact most of the UAE consist of rolling sand dunes of enchanting desert plains, villages and mountains. The mountains situated close to Oman were the main interest, but by default we saw the remote and ancient UAE as seen by the Bedouin tribe. It was these last three aspects our walks focussed on.

We reached the Oman border at 5.00 a.m. with the usual nervousness: we were crossing the border with bottles of beer in the boot, and the border guards were unpredictable.

As we queued up to get our passports stamped, Derek whispered to Talal,

"What about the beer in the car? Will we get into trouble?"

"Maafi Moskilla," said Talal, indicating there would be 'no problem'.

"They are looking for other things," said Ihab.

Geoff, Roy, Derek and myself breathed a sigh of relief. After the climb it was always traditional to have some beers before falling asleep in our tents. After the one hour delay at the border crossing we became conscious of time ticking away as the sun began to rise. We had to climb Jebel Shams today before nightfall and then travel back on the next day (Saturday) to complete the 9 hour journey back to Dubai. The weekend in the Middle East is Friday and Saturday, so work begins on Sunday.

When we reached Fort Sala at 9.30 a.m. the Pajero dashboard was showing an outside temperature of 36 degrees. Surely it was too hot to climb a 3,000 metre mountain.

"It will get cooler when we climb," said Ihab.

"Yeah - early twenties…say twenty-two degrees would suit me fine," I said hopefully.

After an omelette breakfast at a scruffy roadside café, the three cars began to ascend for 30 minutes up the narrow, winding roads that climbed up the base of the mountain. We passed the occasional goatsman's hut. It was a desolate time and forgotten place and it seemed like we had gone back in time. When we parked up the cars at our base camp at 10.00am the temperature gauge declared "22 degrees". My morale was now sky high, as we stretched our legs after this epic car journey. We couldn't wait to start hiking. Our stiff limbs started to loosen up and very slowly the six of us began to walk up the mountain. There was no path but we knew that the route would follow alongside the rim of the Wadi Ghul - which was also known as the Arabian Grand Canyon. When we eventually reached the edge of the canyon after an hour and a half, we were in awe of the spectacular views down the steep sided walls of the edge of the canyon. Standing on the rim, not too close to edge, there was a major drop that must have been somewhere between 300 and a 1000 metres. The six of us just stared at the canyon in amazement: if this was in Europe there would be have been thousands of tourists, eating KFC and taking selfies. Instead there was just six of us here -taking selfies. I had lived in the UAE for three years and I had never heard of the "*Grand Canyon of Arabia*", which is typical for Oman - it was so uncommercialised. I had googled Jebel Shams, and apparently there had been some military battles on these mountain slopes between the the British SAS and communist commandoes back in the 1960s – apparently Ranulph Fiennes had been here in that capacity. We stood and gazed at the steep sided valley beneath and debated what kind a of geological activity must have formed this canyon and the multiple layers of different colours of rock that made the steep sided valley so impressive.

The jagged nature of the rim gave it a fearsome appearance: a gaping hole in the mountain like a giants toothless grin. Roy seemed to take pleasure standing close to the very edge of the rim, with toes reaching the edge, peering down into the abyss: This made me a bit nervous, as the edges were crumbling and unsteady in places.

"How much further to the top?" said Derek.

"The total walk is 3.5 hours so we should be at the top now - which can't be right."

"We are not even halfway there. The peak is somewhere up there," Geoff pointed up the huge mountain before us.

"That means we really need to press on before it goes dark," I said.

The three of us had whipped up enough urgency to continue our ascent. The Arabian grand canyon had been a distraction for forty minutes, and we had underestimated the total duration of the hike by 4 hours: this was time that we didn't have. There were no paths, and head torches were not going to make the rocky, bouldery terrain easier.

As we started walking upwards, Roy had decided to stay at the Grand Canyon, and wait for our return: now there were five of us.

As we ascended the quantities of vegetation become more sparse. The sun was powerful enough to justify wearing a hat for protection and the temperature remained cool. There was a slight breeze at one point, so the weather was perfect. I had my light walking boots on (*Decathalan* specials) which seemed to be okay, but I was concerned about a niggling blister beginning to form on my left foot. With no recognisable path we stepped over small boulders, and most of the ground was dry grit with the occasional bush plant. The five of us were now going at different paces and were strung out over a long distance, so we stopped and sat down on some rocks to take stock. Whilst Talal and Ihab staggered up the mountain, I put a plaster on the blister and changed my wet sweaty socks for a dry pair, and this seemed to do the trick.

"We haven't got much time before dark, so we'll have to up the pace."

Everybody nodded, in between drinking water and nibbling snacks.

"It will be dark at six and we don't want to be coming down the mountain in the dark, without any smooth paths."

"It's going to be really slow descending this mountain using the head torches across these boulders. There's no path. It will be an ankle breaker," said Derek.

"I know, but it would be a shame not to reach the summit when we drove nine hours to get here," I said.

"The mountain is not going anywhere, we can always come back another day," said Derek stretching his legs to stop them from going stiff.

"Okay then it's 1.30 p.m. now - let's agree a cut off point. We turn back at 3 p.m. no matter where we are."

"Okay, it's a deal," I said, realising that the window was small, but at least we had a chance.

We decided to make our packs lighter and leave some bottles of water on a prominent rock together with a spare coat. We still had around one or two litres each which seemed plenty for the next hour or two.

We set off at a faster pace, and I started taking bigger strides to keep up with Geoff and Derek who were around five years older than me, in their early fifties (but probably fitter).

As I placed my foot down on a flat boulder, a snake disappeared behind a rock.

"Watch out for snakes!" I shouted.

The mountain became steeper, and with bent backs we plodded on. Still we could not see the summit. Where was it?

Talal and Ihab had drifted behind.

"We're going to stop here and head back!" shouted Talal.

"Okay, guys, take your time going down!" shouted Geoff, wiping some sweat off his brow with his blue long sleeved top which he wore on every hike.

"Its just us three girls left now," said Derek

We plodded on. This time the pace accelerated. At this stage the conversations had stopped as we conserved energy and we concentrated on keeping up with the pace.

At some point Derek had a complaint about his feet, and shouted up to Geoff and me to carry on. Now there were two of us left.

I was determined to reach the peak. We had driven to another country to climb this mountain and I didn't want to regret a missed opportunity. There was no guarantee we were going to come back and finish off the job. The boulders became larger the nearer we go to the summit, and we heard a strange noise in the distance - somebody calling out, just one word, repeatedly. The noise seemed to coming from the opposite side of the grand canyon, as we were still skirting round the rim.

"What is that noise?"

"Don't know. Could it be a goat farmer who's lost his goat?"

Out of sympathy we made the same noise back which echoed around the mountain.

Eventually, we both finally reached the summit of the Jebel Shams, and we embraced the cool breeze and enjoyed the views of the Hajar mountains. On one side of the peak, another wadhi/grand canyon in front of us, with a sheer drop. Sharing the summit was a military base, which consisted of a white dome shaped building, a large satellite dish and an antenna. It seemed like an odd place for a military base, but at the same time a flat summit, with a dome shaped military base was a perfect place for a bond villian to live.

"Well done mate," I said shaking Geoff's hand. Geoff unveiled his small cotton St. George's flag and we posed for the obligatory pictures, avoiding the military base. We were the only two out of our group of six walkers that had made it to the top. We stood alone, peacefully, admiring the views from the highest mountain in Oman... until we saw a head emerge over the rim of the summit edge, followed by another. Two climbers from New Zealand made their grand entrance to the summit.

We exchanged pleasantries and expressed our surprise to see other climbers using the steepest route on these desolate, crumbling rock faces.

"Come on Gary, we need to go down, just two hours until darkness," said Geoff.

It was so much easier going down but it involved more concentration, especially being sure footed hopping in between the bouldery mountain terrain. The rocks were dry and generally dependable so we built up a reckless pace. After an hour or so I could feel the pressure on my right knee and Geoff was also slowing down. With some luck we found our stash of water and other items that we had discarded on the way up, so we knew we were half way down. We continued our descent and in the semi-darkness we managed to catch up with Ihab and Talal who were steadily limping their way down the mountain. For the last hour we switched on our head torches, but it was painfully slow putting your foot in the right place under the guidance of a flickering light: this was not easy in our state of tiredness. The mountain was now engulfed in complete darkness. When we reached the base camp we limped up to our tents, exhausted both physically and mentally due to the absorbing concentration levels expended on traversing this rugged terrain in the dark. As we put out tents up we were greeted by a reception committee of friendly goats who rummaged through our tents for food as we sat around the camp fire. This was our reward (not the goats) - camping out in Oman was just how camping should be: pitch your tents almost anywhere; little chance of rain; warm air, and no light pollution. The significance of the last point is that in the Arabian Peninsula the clarity and brightest of the stars was like the stars on a christmas card. As the goats continued to rummage for food in our tents, we swapped stories of our different experiences of the day as we ate, smoked and drank beer. It was strange that the two youngest (Talal and Ihab) around their mid-twenties had found the hike most challenging and two of the oldest (Geoff and myself) had completed the trek at a good pace: old people have to cherish these rare victories.

As the night drew on, Derek spoke passionately about the goats and people retired one by one back to their tents, driven by tiredness. It had been a long and glorious day on the mountain of the sun: for us it had been the race against darkness.

THE EIGER TRAIL - JULY 2013

This was a strange trip (and I don't mean a weekend at Glastonbury). Aran and myself had

discussed our next trip to the Alps. I really wanted to have another go at climbing Mont

Blanc, via the Gouter route, but Aran didn't fancy it: it was too crowded and felt as if we

were getting ripped off by the guides. So we decided to go to the Swiss Alps and climb the

Monch (an easy 4000 metre climb) and other stuff around the Grindlewald area. The plan was

that we could do the Swiss Alps without a guide.

Firstly, the logistics were disastrous. Aran drove from London to Geneva and I took a flight

via *Easyjet* from Liverpool to Geneva. Throughout most of the plane journey I was reading

books about climbing the Swiss Alps and also Mont Blanc. I was a like a dog with a bone and

I refused to give up on MB. My flight was delayed by four hours, so Aran waited for me

around Lake Geneva for six hours soaking up the sun until my flight came in.

"Did you buy a map in the airport?" asked Aran.

"No. I forgot." I was loading my rucksack into Aran's car.

"Oh well, we'll get to Grindlewald."

"I have never been to Switzerland before," I said.

We chatted a lot and arrived at an ad hoc camp site and pitched our tent without booking. Our

plan was foiled by a sharp eyed security guard and we were asked to leave.

We had decided to avoid Mont Blanc and to avoid using a guide, as Aran and I were

experienced mountaineers now (arff!).

Aran felt as if Patrick (the French guide that we had used on previous Alpine trips) had been expensive, and that the first two climbs were a bit of a cake walk to beef up the expedition into four days onto the mountain.

"We can buy our own rope and climbing gear, and choose our own routes, like the Monch and the Jungfrau, which are easy."

"Yeah sure, we can do it. Maybe if you can tie me in and do all the technical stuff?"

"Yeah no problem Gaz."

So Aran drove towards Grindelwald and we stopped off at a service station, and slept in the car: when I say "we" it was only Aran that slept in the car and I just lay there with the seat reclined hoping that I would sleep. We planned to set off at 7.00 a.m. but woke up at 09.30 a.m. and Aran started to to drive. Quite soon we received a text off Andy (who was back in the UK) at lunchtime, to said something along the lines of;

"What the F…! You're going the wrong way."

After losing another four hours, Aran turned the car around. The next text from Andy read.

"Are you guys starring in a new flim *Carry on Climbing!"*

As we drove on through the Cote Du Rhone valley, I reminded myself that I must drink more wine from this region as we both sang along to old *New Order* songs.

We stopped off at three supermarkets and a climbing shop, where Aran bought a whopping 100 litre rucksack, some ropes and climbing gear.

"Aran, that's a big rucksack, what are you going to put in a 100 litre rucksack?"

"Er, a lot of food, water and clothes in case we bivvy out."

"What about the rope?"

"Oh we'll take it in turns to carry that."

By the time we arrived at Grindlewald we realised that we had just missed the last train up to the Monch station which would have taken us up to 3800m near the Monch hut.

Having missed the last train of the day (which was a massive blow) we decided to visit the climbing shop and gazed at a huge map of the nearby mountains, and made plans. Which after all is what life is all about about; making plans without actually doing anything.

"We've lost a day," I said.

"Maybe we can walk up the mountain tonight, along the Eiger trail and bivvy under the Eiger," said Aran.

"That sounds good, and that's close to the Eigerstation, so we can get the train up to the Monch station."

Before we left the shop we bought some more expensive climbing gear, in a very expensive Grindlewald.

Aran parked the car near the foot of the Eiger trail and we packed a lot of food (from our three supermarket stops) and water into the rucksacks. Aran had managed to fill his 100 litre rucksack with enough supplies to last a week. As we started to walk uphill, Aran was walking in way that seemed as if the weight was crushing his back, and my rucksack was almost as bad as we walked ever-so-slowly up the zig-zagging path through a forest.

When we stopped for rest, I lifted up Aran's rucksack for entertainment purposes, and felt my old hernia almost popping out.

"Jesus, Mary and Joseph! How many bags of sand are in that?"

"I've got six litres of water and some tins."

"Six litres of water! I've got four litres and that's pushing it," I said.

"Those mountain huts will be charging us 8 Euros per litre. By the way Gaz, its your turn to carry the 100 metres of rope."

"Bloody hell… that's what we used to pay the guide for."

The loop of rope and the clips rattled around and rubbed on my shoulder.

We plodded on for around four or five hours without sight of anybody else on the trail as darkness descended. The path was smooth, and despite carrying a small elephant on our backs, it was a really enjoyable walk. We climbed out of the Grindlewald valley, and saw the tourist town of Grindlewald below, lights twinkling in the dusk. Then straight ahead we could see the Eiger which seemed like a mountain of several kilometres wide. The Eiger Trail now straightened out with the Eiger to our immediate left and Grindlewald at the bottom of the steep valley to our right. It was a classic steep sided valley, and we guessed that we were still only 1,000 metres high.

Darkness descended and we found a spot to bivvy on some very comfortable springy grass/heather. We lay down in the bivvy bags, with our heads poking out of our bivvies staring up at the dark shadowy spectre of the Eiger bearing down at us. The Eiger must have been quite wide as this was only the corner and rest of it stretched out into one long mountain - a massif. The Eiger trail had been a good consolation prize for missing the train and we congratulated ourselves on the successful plan to do a wild camp at the foot of the Eiger. The green grassy slopes of the valley that lead up to the brown rock of the Eiger began to darken rapidly as darkness descended on the valley. Behind us, 1,000 metres at the foot of the valley, Grindlewald was now a cluster of twinkling lights and civilisation seemed far away. It was pitch black all around, and I was enjoying the snugness of the comfortable bivvy. My eyes were alert, as I got to grips with the exposure of wild camping. Despite my aching limbs from carrying the heavy load up the mountain, I could not sleep as I was too busy looking up at the stars. Lying still, on my back, eyes looking upwards I noticed a small beam of light creeping over the top of the Eiger shining down.

"Aran, what's that light on the mountain ridge?"

"Looks like somebody shinning a torch light?"

We both stared at the light and wondered what is was. Maybe we weren't the only people on the mountain.

The torch light gradually became brighter until it formed the shape of the rising moon. A spectacular sight that I had never seen before.

"That's amazing, but spooky."

Lying on my back with the springy grass as a matress, in my cosy bivvy zipped up covering my face, leaving a letter box for my eyes to look up at the mountain and the stars, there was an ambience of peacefulness and contentment with the surroundings that is difficult to reflect in writing. Others, might have described this as some kind of nightmare, but I guess that's why most people live in valleys and not near mountain tops.

I was mesmerised by the majestic sight of the rising moon above the Eiger. It was a surreal experience, even though it was perfectly natural. Chatting quietly and chewing the fat with an old school pal I drifted off to sleep – or perhaps Aran fell asleep before me because I can get quite boring when I am excitedly chattering on about something.

It was the best wild camp I had ever done. Well, its was actually the only wild camp I had ever done. It would take some beating.

What followed was the most comfortable, peaceful nights sleep that I had for days, and little did I know it; for the next few days.

In the morning, we reluctantly moved out of our warm bivvy bags, ate a cold breakfast and packed our rucksacks. For some reason, it always took a long time for me to pack a rucksack. I decided to leave two litres of water hidden in a bush. This weight load was ridiculous and I could hardly lift up my rucksack, and Aran's rucksack was even heavier to the extent that when he rolled hia rucksack onto his back he wobbled as if being hit by a gust of wind.

"What's the rush? It's not as if we have a train to catch," I said teasingly.

"Actually, we do have a train to catch, and it arrives at the Eigerstation stop at 9.00 a.m. and it's 7.40 a.m. now."

"Ahh, 5km in 1 hour 30 minutes, that's easy," I said.

We continued along the Eiger trail which clung to the foot of the Eiger (on the left). This part of the trail possessed a peaceful tranquility; the cheerful birdsong, the lush green grass of the alpine valley slopes to our right. We were the only people on the trail, as it became clear to us that almost everybody would only take the train from Grindlewald. As we passed the north face of the Eiger we gazed up admiringly at this historic mountain and wondered what it would be like to climb this monster. The only man-made sound we could hear was the cow bells chiming nonchalantly, which would only be interrupted by the sound of a distant train coming up the mountain.

"Shit, we have to run," said Aran, lengthening his stride.

"We can't miss it," I said as I started a slow jog, which was only slightly faster that walking. The jogging attempt failed as we carrying the weights of a small rhinoceros on our backs. Five minutes later were sat on the train, surrounded by Japanese tourists taking photographs of the Swiss mountains through the windows. The train would take us to the top of the mountain, where there were viewing platforms, museums and shops. The tourist began to point at our rucksacks with special interest on the ice axes and ropes. It dawned on us that these tourist thought that we were serious mountaineers.

"Are you going to climb the mountains?" said a young Japanese man wearing his brand new North Face coat.

Aran gave me a sideways glance and we played along with the charade.

"Oh yes, we climb," said Aran, and it seemed as if half of the train carriage was now listening to the conversation.

"Will you climb the Eiger?" said another slightly older Japanese tourist wearing a Nike baseball cap.

"Maybe tomorrow," I said, not realising that there was some truth in the answer. However, the answer was good enough, and our two minutes of fame was over.

When the train finally lumbered up to the top of the mountain, we were 140 Euros lighter, and at 3,800 metres high we were also missing oxygen.

As we slowly dodged our way through the crowds, the shops and viewing platform. The cold started to bite; and rather depressingly the mother of all headaches and a feeling of nausea. Travelling up by train was a very quick ascent and we had expected some side-effects. All we had to do was walk one kilometre from the top station to the mountain hut, the Monchhut. It must have taken us almost an hour to do this, as the heavy rucksacks, containing our wild camp gear, food and drink supplies, clothes and climbing equipment resulted in a speed resembling an ageing snail (carrying two other snails on its back).

"Maybe we could do the Monch today if we can just reach the mountain hut so we can stash the supplies and pack a light rucksack," I said.

"It might be too late, looking at the time and condition of the snow at midday," said Aran as he painfully inched forward.

When we reached the hut in a state of hopeless weariness we slumped on the porch and rested in the sun.

"Shall we do a reccy out there?" I said, and looked at Aran who was already asleep, snoring gently, whilst in a sitting position. After a few hours badly needed sleep we sat in the Monch hut dining hall, at one of the long wooden, communal tables. Our plan was to get up at 5.00a.m. and climb the Monch (4,000m) which was situated only 200 metres from the hut, without a guide. It seemed like a straightforward climb.

During dinner some conversations were in English, and then Aran began waxing lyrical in French to fellow climbers on the table, and I couldn't understand much of the conversation so I just watched the faces of each person who was talking. I was like a puppy watching a washing machine go round and round. After dinner, Aran turned to me.

"Gaz, I've just struck a deal with a guide who is free for the next two days. He can take us up the Monch, Jungfrau and the Frauch 300 Euros all-in. We start tomorrow. We get up at 4.30."

"Aran, well done mate. I wondered what you were waffling on about in French."

"We are lucky his two Amercian clients dropped out as they weren't feeling up to it."

"Does the guide know our… standard… you know, our capabilities?"

"Just make sure you do as the guide says,"said Aran

"Ah okay, I must have the reputation of a rebel."

"Just be on form and prepare your gear tonight. Light and bare essentials."

I enthusiastically packed my rucksack whilst in a state of mild excitement, removing a surprisingly large quantity of food and drink – there was enough to supply a small african village - plus additional layers of clothing. My surplus gear filled two large plastic trays. On a wave of excitement I trotted off to bed, in the communal dormitory with a dozen other snoring mountaineers. I wondered what the next day would bring and if I was capable of climbing these new mountains.

At 5.00 a.m. Aran's alarm went off and there wasn't much activity of people getting ready, just a low murmuring of disappointed voices in French and German. Something was wrong. Somebody opened the curtains and all we could see was a blanket of white and grey haze. I got up and took a closer look, almost pressing my face against glass. Yes, it was fog, thick fog.

"Oh no. That's bad news." I said.

"I'll check with the guide to see what the weather situation is."

Aran returned after ten minutes.

"This low cloud is set for two days. None of the guides are taking anybody out in this visbility."

For the rest of the day, we sat in the hut and discussed the weather with around thirty other climbers, in thirty different languages. There were only three options; either (i) take the train back down to Grindlewald, meaning that it cost another 140 Euros to come back up or (ii) stay in hut for two days watching the fog, waiting for a random guide to turn up, or (iii) find an easy walk/climb around the nearby glacier near the hut.

Options (i) and (ii) were expensive, and option (iii) was really fumbling around in the dark. This was alpine climbing at its worst; sitting around waiting for good weather/decent snow conditions. After a lengthy British style debate, a plan emerged.

We were at 3,800 metres and the low cloud was sat on top of us. If the cloud base was at 3,000 metres and if we travelled down the mountain to the Eigerstation, at 2,400 metres there should be no cloud, and we could climb the via ferrata on the Eiger. Brilliant plan. We took the train down below the cloud to the Eigerstation which was basking in sun. The weather here was in complete contrast to the icy, pea soup Monchstation. Once again we walked down the Eiger trail and scanned the rocks to see where the vertical iron ladders were situated. We stopped to have lunch at a picnic table below the Eiger, amongst the tourists and families and we noticed two people climbing up the ladders fixed against the rocks to the right of the north face of the Eiger.

Everybody was wearing shorts and t-shirts. It was sun tan weather.

"This looks great Aran, but I've never done a via ferrata before."

"Dead easy Gaz, we put on our climbing harnesses and use some makeshift slings with karabiners to clip into the harness at one end and another clip to clip into the iron vertical pole. There is only two things that can go wrong; one, you forget to clip into the iron pole next to the ladders or two, the vertical pole somehow gives way and breaks and you end up being the latest Eiger victim."

"It would probably make the Daily Mail. Forty Seven year old British climber falls to his death off the Eiger," I said.

"But today's news is tomorrow's fish and chip paper."

The via Ferrata consisted of sections of vertical ladders, which provided a route over the Eiger. The route started around 200 metres to the right of the north face, but we had no idea where the route ended up. We started off going up the ladders slowly, and soon we gained height and obtained a large dose of exposure. The cliff was almost vertical so I was gripping the rungs of the ladder. Aran was moving much more quickly. The gap lengthened between us.

"Gaz, what are you doing?"

"I've got this system, where I'm clipped in twice. I brought an extra sling so I thought I'd use it."

"Shove it in your rucksack, Gaz. You only need to be clipped in once. We can't hang around, those clouds from the Monchstation are lowering down onto us."

I looked up and saw that the sun was becoming less fierce and the sky was becoming pale and milky.

We continued up the ladders, but this time with less chatter as we had read about the unpredictable and severe weather changes that plagued climbers on the Eiger.

When we were around a few hundred metres high, the temperature started to drop and I had stopped looking down because that was not helping me overcome my fear of heights.

Instead I became fascinated with the North face of the Eiger to the left of the ladders. The north face seemed very close and the vertical angle of the cliffs looked impossible to climb.I kept glancing over again and again at the north face; It was so steep I couldn't imagine anybody climbing it – even though its legendary stories such as the *White Spider* had detailed these climbs in graphic detail. For me, the ladders was enough exposure.

I remained on autopilot going up the ladders, as my feet plodded up the rungs like a mouse on a treadmill and my hands gripped the cold metal rungs ever so tightly as I gained more height. The only time I had to think was when the ladders section came to an end and I had to adjust the clip onto a new section. Aran broke the silence and shouted out.

"Gaz, the ladders have run out."

I didn't believe Aran so I climbed up the next section of ladders to where Aran was waiting,

"Where's the next section of ladders? I said panting.

"There are no ladders now."

I looked up at a ladderless slope above us. It was very steep, around 50 degrees.

"Unbelievable, fuckin unbelievable. A via ferratta which runs out of ladders half way up the Eiger."

"Maybe it had become loose and fallen off the cliff."

"The guy in front must have cleared this section safely, so I guess we should try."

"Yeah, we've come this far, no point in turning back."

"I'll go first, but leave a gap in case I slip."

"Yep, one slip and it's good night Vienna."

Aran started to scramble up the ladderless slope, unroped and unladdered without saying anything as he went.

As I followed there were some small footholds. I emphasise the word "small", as they were more like small dints in the rock face, which the toe could purchase some grip on. The problem was that the surface was a mixture of rock, dirt and grit, and then the footholes disappeared. I looked around for obvious holds but there were none. I wasn't going to hang around on a slope that seemed near vertical and began to increase the speed of my legs to move up this section quickly. As I continued upwards silently cursing the crumbling gritty surface, I kicked my toes into the dry dirt to create some small dust clouds around my feet. In the middle of the section I gripped my finger nails hard into the surface. Soon, I could see Aran clipping onto the next ladder section and I clung on to the safety of the ladder. We both paused for a couple of minutes to regain our composure.

"Jesus Christ, that was scary," Aran said.

"I hope we don't have to go down this route. That would be impossible."

As we continued upwards the route was impressively close to the north face to the left of the via Ferrata – there were no climbers on the north face today. We noticed the colour of the rock becoming darker, and the light changing.

"Shit, look at those clouds above us."

"They are sinking fast," I said as I put my waterproof coat on, and Aran followed suit.

We carried straight up to the top of the cliff which was about two thirds of the height of the north face and then we seemed to go onto a plateaux before going up another section.

We look up and around to see the German climber in front of us, but there was no sign of him anywhere. Little did we know that we should have gone to the right and and climbed the "Rostock" peak.

If the first section was like a summer climb, then the next section was more of autumn climb as the rocks were wet with mist, and there were patches of frost. The landscape was a bit like the "Devil's Kitchen" or "Bristly ridge" on the Glyder range in Wales. Wet, misty with strangely shaped rock pinnacles. As the dark clouds circled above us, there was certainly a storm brewing. A wicked wind began whip across our faces, and it was difficult to believe we had started this climb in perfect summer conditions in shorts and T-shirts.

Aran began a frantic pace and I followed as fast as I could, clearing ladder after ladder. Clipping and and unclipping. Forty five minutes ago I was a novice via ferrata climber and now I felt like a veteran. The cliffs became very steep again, but we didn't have time to look around at the water gushing down from the rocks. Small streams were pouring down from our right and my gloves were soaked, icy cold.

"Bloody hell it's freezing. I need to get another layer on," I said. We both stopped and fumbled in our rucksacks and while I was fastening my straps Aran was already tearing up the next section.

"Gaz, there is a real storm brewing up and we don't want to be on this rock face in thunder and lightning, with water gushing down on top of us."

A couple of minutes later we were nearly at the top of the next ridge and it started to hail. Pieces of ice the size of a small coins were hammering down on our faces from above. The ladders became slippy and the rockface was covered in small ice pellets blowing violently around the rock face. Hail stones poured down directly into our faces and the rickety set of ladders didn't help. I was having problems seeing my hands because my eyes were blinking instinctively to shut out the stinging hail stones. The changing weather front on the Eiger was something I have never seen on a mountain before – it was so sudden and violent. There was something eerie about the instantaneous change in weather conditions. The gusts of wind thundered across the rock face creating a howling noise. It was so dramatic, like a 1950s, black and white horror movie. It was almost like the mountain was alive and angry. Small rivers of hail began to fall down the rock face and I wondered how long this hellish storm would last. It was a huge relief when the hail had finished; then I could open my eyes fully and see where I was going, which is always an advantage when climbing up a mountain. I was beginning to feel that we had bitten off more than we could chew, when we eventually reached the summit ridge - or what we thought was the summit (the real summit was Rostock, that we had bypassed by accident). In from of us and below we could see the Eigerglacier in its full glory, sweeping down the mountain side; a giant river of ice and snow. It was a huge basin, and it was quite a surprise to find this view on the other side of the mountain, although I'm not sure what we were expecting. There were no climbers in sight and no ladders going down the steep cliff that lead the boulder field, but after a while we noticed a metal rope clinging to a 15 metre section of cliff, and realised it was the only way down and slowly abseiled down the cliff. The abseil was not Bear Grylsian but more Eddie the eagle. After this part, our feet were firmly on the ground and it just a matter of jumping from boulder to boulder to work our way down the mountain slopes that were on the opposite side of the mountain that we started on. This slope would eventually arch back towards the railway track. As a walker, I was now on familiar ground skipping across the rocks and boulders. The rocks were dry, no wind, no storm; another completely different weather front. As we neared the end of the circuit near the railway track, It was difficult to take in all of the drama that had just unfolded such a short time ago. The bouldering stretch was good fun, and as we reached the track my heartbeat had resumed its normal pace. I felt like the via ferrata had been a real roller coaster; completely unpredictable – a white knuckle ride. We walked along the railway track and looped back round to the Eiger to pick up our climbing gear that we had stashed behind some rocks. Next came a well rewarded break as we sat down on a bench and began to eat our lunch whilst we gazed up at the Eiger. The clouds continued to lower down over the mountain, a clear signal that the show was over. As we grappled with our heavy rucksacks, Aran was complaining about pain in his knee. He rummaged through his 100 litre rucksack and decided to make some serious choices about the weight, and to my amazement he pulled out a large tin of rice pudding.

"I think I can survive without that for the next few hours," said Aran and he reluctantly placed the tin on the wooden bench. We both laughed at the ridiculous weights we were carrying.

We slowly trotted along the Eiger trail away from the railway line, but this time moving downhill towards Grindlewald, with the clouds following us all the way. Once again there was not another soul on this route.

When we reached the car park the slate grey clouds had darkened and were descending into the valley. It started to rain, and it looked like a storm was brewing.

We set up the tent in the car park and as the rain poured down we opened up some tins of French beer.

When the morning came, the weather had got worse and the car park was full of large puddles. It was still raining. And I was getting fed up.

"What are we going to do? No guide, no plan and no weather." I said.

"We go into Grindlewald, get a guide and go up on the train tomorrow and do the Monch the day after."

"How much is that going to cost?" I said as the rain water dripped down my nose.

"140 Euros for the train, 120 euros for the hut for a couple of days, 200 Euros for the guide…"

I was thinking that I only had one week left of my vacation, and my wife and three kids were waiting for me in the UK basking in sun and sleeping in comfortable beds, eating good food.

"And there is no guarantee of decent weather. We might end up just sitting in the Monchhut again."

"Well, this *is* mountaineering," said Aran as he rolled up the wet tent.

"I'm not sure I like it. We're both unorganised, the plan keeps on changing, and the weather is crap. If I see that tin of rice pudding again I'll throw myself off the via ferrata. Let's call it a day."

The two drowned rats drove back to Geneva. It was well sign posted. That was our last trip to the Alps.

THE STAIRWAY TO HEAVEN - FEBRUARY 2014

The "Stairway To Heaven" is the most exciting and the most dangerous hike in the UAE. It is situated near the highest mountain (Jebel Jais), in the Wadhi Ghalilah. In total, it's a 17km route which includes a walk and climb up a 1,500 metre cliff. To be honest, this cannot be described as a "trek" or a "hike"; it's more of a climb, and a white knuckle ride across crumbling cliffs. There is some high grade scrambling involved, and its unsuitable for people suffering from vertigo. The last factor should have been enough to put me off.

When I was working in the United Arab Emirates, my work colleague and friend Geoff introduced me to a group of ex-pat hikers who made regular trips into the mountains of the northern Emirates in places like Rhas Al Khaimah (RAK), or Fujariah. Geoff organised the trips, and word got round the office and all kinds of people turned up at the rendezvous, in various states of fitness and clothing. Walking in the mountains and wadhis of RAK or Fujairah was truly an "adventure" as there were no signposted paths, no mountain rescue service and generally no people around. Some of the favourite circular routes we named ourselves such as "Camp Macleod", "The Witch's Nose" and "Smith's Rambunctious Ridge Walk". I have to add that Geoff named most of these walks: ridge walks were favourites regardless of the quality of crumbling ridge rocks. On the Witch's Nose - which was a hike through a wadhi in Fujairah that lead into another wadhi - the entrance was marked by a rock shaped like a witch's head. The walks did not always end well, and this was the location where a newbie hiker, who was more of an old newbie, turned up looking pale and carrying a lot of timber as if he hadn't left his sofa in twenty years. He managed to twist his ankle near the Witch's Nose and we aborted the walk to limp back to the car. The next day he was on crutches, off work for three weeks, and after that... we never saw him again.

Having said all of the above, for many hikers in the UAE the most talked about walk was the "Stairway to Heaven" - and it wasn't for novices. Even now, just looking at the photographs of the Wadhi Gallilah and its precipitous cliffs – it still gives me the butterflies.

Geoff, Derek and myself had done some walks up to the start of the Stairway itself, which was approximately two hours along a well trodden path at the foot of the valley (Wadhi Gallilah). We would walk up to the cliff face of the stairway which marked the end of the cul-de-sac valley. As we munched on our sandwiches we would stare up at the towering cliffs and eventually exhaust all possible descriptions; "It's massive", "the cliffs are bloody vertical", "it will be a tough climb" and then Derek would say "this chicken tikka sandwich is amazing, especially with a touch of mayo." Whilst Derek was appreciating the products from the kitchen of the *Emirates* petrol station, Geoff was looking for the routes up the cliffs; the hidden stairways. It was an enigma - a puzzle that Geoff was determined to crack. Derek and myself were happy to turn up on time, with reasonable gear and good quality sandwiches and follow Geoff up the mountain. If Geoff wasn't there I doubt there would have been a credible stairway ascent. We were anxious to avoid another grim headline story in the Emirates news – it was bad for tourism, and that would make the Shiekh very angry.

Geoff had previously made an attempt at the stairway and retreated halfway, because Geoff and his climbing partner had simply run out of time; they got stuck on the ledges and were unable to find the stairway steps. They had burnt up precious time, as they burn up in the desert sun. They were also low on water and had to get off the mountain before darkness. It was a downward spiral of having to move, but not having the strength to walk. They slowly and painfully reached their car four hours later in the dark, dehydrated and exhausted. Geoff's partner (Roy) was having problems walking straight. Apparently when they drove thirty km from the mountain they both staggered into a medical facility, also known as *Kentucky Fried Chicken*; the *Colonel* had reached out and provided ample injections of sugar, salt, protein and water. It's difficult to image how people survived before these essential community services were established. The story had become an epic in the *Wanderer's* bar, and Derek was particularly interested in the *KFC Royale*.

Joking apart, this was a tough old climb, and Geoff had his first taste of it, and wanted to go back for the family bucket. Over the next couple of years Geoff began plotting the locations of the hidden stairways on his GPS, until he was confident he could have a proper crack at it and return this time without the colonel. Geoff was a great organiser of mountain trips. His preparation for kit was methodical and well thought out. An endearing part of Geoff's character was that he had a remarkable patience for people like me who weren't organised, but maybe this provided a source of entertainment. I usually ended up forgetting some item of kit (a hat, suncream, or a walking pole). Geoff sometimes spread out his mountaineering kit on the floor and photographed it. At home he probably had all of his books filed in alphabetical order. As you can see, I'm jealous, and I need to, and do, welcome organised people into my world like Geoff and Andy. When we get two unorganised people like me and Aran the pathway to disaster slowly unravels.

The big day of the stairway trip had finally arrived. Without trying to go into hyperbole on this trip, it was our biggest walk (I really mean walk/climb; God, this is confusing) that we had done, and were ever likely to do, in the UAE. This was the UAE cup final of walks/hikes/treks/climbs (sorry - now I am really rambling on and on).

We had carefully chosen a February day and the downside was that we had less daylight hours but the massive upside was the cooler temperatures, so there was less scope for dehydration. Dehydration or sun stroke would take away our ability to climb or walk steadily, and both of these factors would be needed to come back in one piece.

At 5.00 a.m. Geoff, Derek and myself waited at a petrol station somewhere in Sharjah, and Gabrielle and James joined us from Dubai. Eventually we left Sharjah at 5.30 a.m, and two hours later our three jeeps arrive at the mountainous Emirate of Rhas Al Khamaih. The 4x4 vehicles were necessary to go across 10km across dirt tracks to reach to foot of the valley, and the *Jeep* brand was also necessary for your image as an ex-pat. Once we parked up, it must have taken twenty five minutes for everybody to pack their rucksacks, get their boots on, and generally fiddle and faff around with gear. Most people had three lires of water, but I always took four, so I had an extra litre. My rucksack contained only water, food and a light waterproof coat and it was not much bigger than an alpine day pack. I also had my NASA survival bag, which was a poor man's bivvy bag made out of a polythene and tin foil (it folded up to the size of a Mars bar and weighed less. For once, I was ready. I had tentatively packed my rucksack the night before with greater care than usual. This was a serious expedition. I guessed the more people in the walking party, the longer it would take. I noticed that James didn't seem to have much walking gear and looked like he was dressed to go for a walk on the beach: I wondered if he was going to struggle. It was must have been around 7.45

a.m. by the time the group of five hikers set off along the well trodden path down the Wadhi. It was a 10 hour trek so we were against the clock once more. Geoff was already anxiously looking at his watch. We set off at a brisk pace to get warm as it was a cool thirteen during the early morning, with temperatures set to peak at around twenty-five degrees in the cooler mountains. Five minutes into the walk, we hit our first delay.

"Oh shit, I've forgot my camera!" said Gabrielle as she ran back to her car, disappearing into the dim dawn light. It was already 8.00 a.m. and I was getting a bit twitchy. Eventually we reached the end of the Wadhi Galilah and we were confronted with the imposing sight of the stairway cliff face in front of us. We moved quickly past a large square shaped boulder the size of a house at the foot of the valley across various other car sized boulders and Derek decided to stash some of his water behind some rocks to lighten his load, and I also left some items as peace offerings to the mountain gods.

As we climbed up to the first ledge, we looked up at the imposing cliff above us. I turned round and looked down at the house boulder, which now looked much smaller. Geoff walked ahead holding his GPS in front of him, and as if by magic we found the first stairway up to the next level. We knew that this was where the adventure really started. The steps were made from a series of small loose boulders. Shoeless tribesman had built the makeshift steps up the cliff, but it is not clear why they did this. One theory was that the route was a means of meeting or attacking the neighbouring tribes who lived at the top of the cliffs.

The mountain has claimed several lives, and many injuries. In 2012, an adventure had a sickening end when a 31-year-old British pilot (who worked for Emirates Airlines) fell 1,000 metres to his death from a narrow pathway. It was around this time when we were planning on making the trip, and most people in the ex-pat community considered the climb as sheer madness.

There was no marked route up the stairway, no guide books with GPS tracked routes and no mountain rescue service. Also there was no National Trust or climbing clubs responsible for maintaining the paths. Commercial climbing tours stopped taking people up the stairway for these reasons, and the major difficulties of taking injured people off the cliffs to receive medical care.

In 2011, an Australian climber lost his footing and fell head-over-heals onto a ledge, breaking his leg. The group of 17 climbers called for help and within 1 hour there were twenty people from other climbing groups around the UAE on their way to RAK to help bring the injured climber down the mountain. During that day, they could not move him down the cliffs. The next day more volunteers were rounded up from the climbing community and it took them 6 hours to lower the injured man down from the mountain, section by section by either just ropes, or by stretcher depending on the width of each ledge. The entire rescue took longer than twenty hours.

Meanwhile, everything was going to plan for the five us; we were making good progress up the stairway, and Geoff's GPS locations seemed to work a treat. Everybody seemed sure footed and comfortable with the staircases, but we knew that at least five staircases were almost vertical. I had one major fear at the back of mind, and it was famous narrow ledge that had to be traversed whilst clinging on to a rugged rock face, which had overhangs just to make it more difficult… and, oh yes, there was a sheer drop below of several hundred metres. Geoff had crossed it on his previous stairway attempt and said the width of the ledge varied from six inches to one foot, depending on who he was trying to impress. Geoff had told this story several times, and it was etched in my mind. It was another Gran Paradiso nightmare ledge coming back to haunt me. These narrow ledges always had a *bloody* overhanging rock to make your arse hang over the ledge - to make them even more scary.

As we reached around halfway up the cliff we stepped above the cool shadow that was covering the botton half of the valley. We felt the sun on our backs for the first time that day. It was a nice feeling to touch warm limestone, although some fragments had crumbled and fallen loose, evidenced by the debris scattered on the ledges. As we walked along the ledge looking for the steps, occasionally we could see small cairns next to the steps, and I picked up a small stone and placed it on the cairn every time I passed, to try and help the next party. I become aware that our party of five were the only people on the mountain, or the valley approach. We were the only group on the stairway, surrounded by bright limestone cliffs, with the occasional rakish tree, which somehow (by coincidence) seemed to mark the next set of steps. Walking up the steps was a strange experience, as each was unique in its own construction.

The stories in the media that were less talked about was the difficulty of completing the hike within ten or eleven hours, which was probably the average time for completion. Most of the distance was walking along the valley to the stairway cliffs and back, which was probably about four hours as the paths were quite level and easy to follow. After that the tricky part was ascending and descending the towering cliffs, and not getting lost. The disaster scenario, apart from falling off, was getting stuck on the cliffs overnight. At the time of writing the Stairway was outside the KFC delivery zone.

We continued the routine of tentatively ascending the stairways and making good progress onto the next levels. It was only when we walked along the narrow ledges did we gain appreciation of the height and exposure around us. The stairways were ancient and made out of lots of small and crumbling rocks. They were the key to avoid being trapped on a ledge with no way up, or no way down. The consequence of not locating each stairway resulted in climbers wandering up and down the ledges searching for the next set of stairways. The wandering distances were anything between a few metres to a couple of hundred metres until you found the hidden crumbling stairway going up to the next level. It was a mountaineer's *Donkey Kong* game. The stairs had been hand made by the tribesmen in the same pale rock colour as the cliff face, and in the bright sunlight it was difficult not to continuously walk past the hidden stairs and start to curse repeatedly until the next set of stairs could be found.

Around three quarters of the way up we encountered the famous narrow ledge, the moment I had been dreading. The ledge was not straight, it curved, and at one point an overhanging rock coincided with a narrowest part of the ledge which looked like six or eight inches at one point, although I didn't stop to measure it – let's just say it was bloody narrow. Geoff shuffled across, sideways like a crab facing the cliff face as he went. Gabrielle followed with her back to the ledge (for some reason) facing outwards, like Spider Woman. James came next, using a combination of the first two techniques, repeatedly muttering to himself how beautiful the texture of the rock was (I guess that flattery gets you everywhere). Then it was my turn, and I genuinely did not know which technique to use, knowing that the more I deliberated the more wobbly my legs would become.

"If this ledge was 3 metres above the ground, we wouldn't even be bothered about this," said Derek as he waited for his turn. Heights play tricks on your brain and cause fear, anxiety and vertigious feelings. Those feelings are fine when you are tied into a rope as protection. As I shuffled sideways across the 3 metre ledge of death, I held both hands up above me groping for the rock, trying to ignore the fact that I had a 1,000 metre cliff face below me. I was so busy concentrating on not tripping over my own shuffling feet that my hands couldn't find any hand holds, and I didn't know whether to look up or down, so I did both. At the most difficult section with the overhang my hands just caressed the rock when there were no handholds, effectively helping the balance. Alas It was all footwork, and my moves were baby steps rather than strides, so the agony was prolonged. The initial small sideways shuffles to the right were replaced with wider strides as I lost patience and just wanted to get the dangerous traverse over and done with. It happened so quickly that the wobbly disco legs never made it to the dance floor. The smooth and polished rock sloped downwards at one point. As I stepped on onto the wider ledge, my relief was tangible. All five of us were across safely.

"Imagine what that would have been like on the wet slippy rocks of Snowdonia," I said with some relief, as we climbed up the next set of vertical stairs.

"We just have to cross that ledge once more on the way back as I don't know the circular route around the rim and down the other cliffs," said Geoff, who was clearly sticking with the plan.

"It's a pity we didn't take some video footage, because everybody had a different technique of traversing that ridge," I said.

Thirty minutes later we reached the top of the Stairway To Heaven. We sat down on the stoney plateau the size of a small football pitch (it was a most unusual peak) and began eating our sandwiches. There was a goat farm on the plateau, but our main interest was the incredible view of the valley (Galillah Wadhi) below us. It was another grand canyon, but this time it was the grand canyon of the UAE. I couldn't take my eyes off the many layers of rock strata that formed the 1,500 metre cliff face around the valley. The scale and beauty of the towering cliffs were an awesome sight that the photographs could only partially capture. As I peered over the edge, it was sheer drop down the vertical cliff face that made my legs wobble.

As we tucked into our sandwiches and topped up on water I realised that I consumed two and half litres already without having to pee. This was typical in the desert climate; you sweated the water out of your body.

"The job's only half done, we have to go down the same way."

"You know how to take all the fun out of a summit celebration, " I said.

"We've got fifteen minutes left and then we can take our time going down," said Geoff, checking his watch.

At this point a goats herdsman wandered up to us, and we greeted him.

"Sabah, Keefalak!"

"Zen. Alhamdelah Zen," said the goat farmer with a beaming smile, a white dish dash, and his red and white head scarf. The farmer handed out some bottles of water to us, and we handed him some chocolate and some Coca-Cola.

"Shukran," said the farmer as he sat amongst us.

It was perfectly natural to be welcomed in this way in the rural parts of the UAE. The old Bedouin culture still prevailed, which was based on welcoming travelling guests with food, water and shelter. It was a humbling experience for us every time, and was completely different to the UK where farmers or landowners could provide a hostile welcome to visitors. For me, the Arabic culture was at its most impressive in the rural parts where we had seen this generousity every time we made a remote camp or stopped to take a rest near some farm or village during our hikes in Fujairah or RAK. On one occasion on the East coast of Fujairah a local had seen our camp fire from the village some miles below and driven up in his 4x4 with trays of cooked food and drinks which he handed out enthusiastically. Unfortunately the cooked food looked like semolina and contained chicken strips, which tasted like mucus, and he sat there intently watching us eating it very slowly – we smiled politely, and he seemed satisfied. We never found out the true ingredients – perhaps its better that way.

Meanwhile back on the plateau above the stairway, we exhausted our limited supply of Arabic words and wished the goat farmer "Naharak Sayeed" (have a nice day).

I wondered how many visitors he received living on top of a 1,500 metre cliff, where the only access was up the stairway or the long drive across the mountains to the nearest coast road. As we carefully descended the stairways we were very optimistic about completing the expedition before nightfall. When we crossed the narrow ledge again, it seemed much easier, and I really don't know why. It was either some familiarity or practice makes perfect or quite simply that it was more of a right handed grip as we traversed the ledge. Going down the vertical stairways was slower, due to the loose stones that made up the steps and handholds. The human body is more suited to ascents that descents and that is probably why most accidents happen going down the mountains.

Time began to tick away, and the challenge of finding hidden stairways became more difficult, resulting in walking back and to across ledges, and peering over the cliffs. Sometimes we split up, so the five of us spread out across the ledge.

"Here it is!" shouted James, who appeared to enjoy standing very close to the crumbling edges.

The novelty of finding hidden steps soon began to wear off, with us gettting stuck on one particular level for twenty minutes. Luckily, we had built up some contingency with our rapid ascent, so it did not prove to be a gamechanger.

When five sets of aching, creaky knees reached the bottom of the stairway, we collected our stash of water, and the relief amongst the team was obvious for all to see. As we headed off down the level valley path, we looked up at the giant vertical cliff face and the stairway to heaven.

"It's difficult to believe that we were on top of that cliff two hours ago," I said, proudly. Heaven and back in the same day.

"Great walk, pity about my sandwich though, Chicken was a bit tough," said Derek.

"It was probably goat meat," said Geoff

* * * * *

MOUNT KENYA

Six Day Diary of the Mount Kenya Expedition (16.10.2016 - 22.10.2016)

Introduction

Before we start the six-day diary, let's cover some background information about Mount Kenya.

Mount Kenya (5199m) is the second highest mountain in Africa and despite its close proximity to Kilimanjaro it is relatively unknown. For me, this unknown entity was a good enough reason to "discover" Mount Kenya. Kilimanjaro stands at 5895m as the highest mountain in Africa, and for many hikers it's part of the international bucket list of accessible peaks. I've spoken to so many people who have climbed Kilimanjaro, that I feel like I have climbed it myself.

The Mount Kenya Massif is a dormant volcano, consisting of several peaks including Batian (5199m), Nellion (5188m) and Lenana (4985m). The first two are climbing peaks and the third, Lenana, is a trekking peak. The Lenana peak was the focus and objective of our six day expedition.

Commercial hiking operators offer three main routes to the Lenana peak: The Sirimon route (two days' ascent - the quick and dirty route), Chogoria route (four days' ascent - the gradual acclimatisation route) and the Burguret route (five days' ascent – a long wilderness route for the intrepid explorer). We had opted for Chogoria route on the ascent and Sirimon route on the descent, and we had no regrets.

All of the three peaks are named after the Masai tribal chiefs. The Masai tribe consisted of fierce warriors and cattle herdsman who were superstitious about the peaks of Mount Kenya. Up until fifty years ago, the Masai would only venture as far as the northern slopes as the peaks were perceived as being the "throne of the Gods."

The first European pioneers who discovered the mountain in the 1840s, took decades to agree that snow and ice could actually exist on the equatorial peaks. Joseph Johnson, who was tasked by the Royal Geographical Society (RGS) in 1885 to "examine" the mountain famously said, "*he who goes gently, goes safely, he who goes safely, goes far*".

The great Scottish mountaineer, Halford Mackinder, accompanied by Hausberg the photographer, conquered the Batian summit in 1899. However, Mackinder's long journey to the summit was littered with challenges of epic proportions. It had taken 19 days walking to reach the high camp, and along the way they faced several disasters : a small pox epidemic in Mombasa (resulting in quarantine), a rail crash from which they emerged unscathed and another small pox epidemic in Nairobi. As if this wasn't enough, the 170 porters recruited on the coast could not bear the cold in the higher ground so they deserted in dribs and drabs and were gradually replaced by fewer, but tougher Masai tribesmen and Italian guides. However, Mackinder's ongoing problem was that he was unable to obtain supplies due to a local famine. They endured ambushes from tribes, attacks from rhinos, and a grass fire (started by a discarded match). The summit attempt was finally made possible by Gorges (a member of

Mackinder's party) who brought desperately needed rations and supplies to Mackinder at the high camp, two hours before Mackinder was prepared to turn back. For his gratitude, the widest valley to east was named "Gorges valley".

Felice Benuzzi was fascinated by Mount Kenya, because each day it formed a spectacular view from his home - a P.O.W camp at Nayuki, where he was held captive by the British soldiers during World War II. The Italian plotted his escape from the POW camp but his main objective was to climb the mountain. He based his route on the map of Mount Kenya that featured on the label of an Oxo tin. Many fellow prisoners were convinced that Benuzzi's plan to escape and climb Mount Kenya was mad due to the lack of resources, equipment, and available food. Two others (a doctor and a sailor) eventually joined him in the plot to escape. They improvised to make ropes and crampons from pieces of bedding and they saved what they could from the food rations.

The foothills were infested with big game and they were unarmed. Their encounters with the animals are some of the most exciting passages in the story. They also battled against illness, hunger, and freezing temperatures on their ascent to the Lenana summit where they proudly placed the Italian flag.

Eighteen days after leaving the camp they returned, driven by fatigue and hunger. The British commandant sent the escapees into solitary confinement for 30 days, but later reduced this to seven days, as a "sporting gesture". Controversy continued when in 1943 the British press reported the great Italian adventure, but they claimed that the Italians' flag had been mounted on the peak upside down. The Italians denied that they had placed their flag upside down. However In the whole scheme of things, this was just semantics. Regardless of the position of the flag, it was a remarkable adventure by the Italians. Benuzzi later wrote a detailed and gripping account of the escape (*"No Picnic on Mount Kenya"*) which is regarded as one the great mountain adventure stories of all time. It is testament to the human spirit of rebellion, stamina, and resourcefulness.

The mountain has a rich history of adventures. Now it was time for my own adventure.

Six Day Diary of the Mount Kenya Expedition (16.10.2016 - 22.10.2016)

Day One. Heron Portico Hotel (Nairobi)

Six hikers from the UK (Nigel, Liz, Sally, Graham, Geoff, and myself) squeezed into an old Land Cruiser for the 150km journey from Nairobi to Mount Kenya. We soon got to know our fellow hikers on the road out of Nairobi city. The journey became more scenic as we traversed across the flat equatorial lands, which hosted a rich variety of agriculture fields. Kenya looked like a bright and colourful place, especially on this Sunday morning with local people walking to church in their Sunday best. The 1970s Toyota started a gentle climb up to the foothills of Mount Kenya. The surprisingly comfortable Land Cruiser still "had legs", although it was probably on its last legs. At one point the heavily laden vehicle spluttered to a halt about 100 meters short of reaching the top of a large hill. Our guides from the Tour Company (KE Adventure) gave us the opportunity to stretch our legs (literally) by asking for volunteers to push the old beast up the hill for a jump start. It worked.

After lunch we left the tarmac road and we switched cars. Our party of six split up into two groups of three in each Land Rover. Both Land Rovers were old - this time 1980s vintage. They faithfully chugged along the ascending dirt track through the bamboo forest. When the track became too steep it was difficult to guess who would collapse first, the old Land Rover or the passengers inside choking on diesel fumes. Nevertheless, we were lucky to hitch a ride through the foothills, as it had taken a couple weeks for early explorers to hack through the bamboo jungle to get this far. We started to hike the last 5km to the mount Kenya lodges (2730m) and Graham spotted some water buffalo and monkeys roaming in the valley (at a safe distance). Welcome to Africa.

Day Two.

The next morning, just before sunrise Geoff reported that various animals were wandering around the huts; antelope (I was still asleep and missed them), water buffalo (they were too far away when I emerged from the hut) and finally colobus monkeys (I chased them with camera in hand like a desperate tourist). The only attraction (not hiding away from sight) was the spectacular Mount Kenya Massif spread out across most of the panorama, with the majestic African trees in the foreground. It was definitely Africa.

I was surprised to find so many porters waiting to start the expedition. There were around 15 porters getting ready to carry the party's food, tent, and camp baggage, and they set off first carrying their loads, including various pieces of furniture. I was used to carrying my own gear in the Alps, so I felt slightly guilty about the porters carrying my kit bag, but I learned to live with it. The guilt increased further when we spotted a square white plastic garden table (our dinner table apparently) strapped to a porter's back. It was the type of table you would find outside a café. This made a peculiar sight. Man and table marched ahead in the distance.

This spectacle created some bemusement amongst the six British hikers, making us feel like spoilt Victorian colonials. Maybe the Victorian climbers had insisted on this type of furniture during the Mackinder expedition, and it had stayed on the 'essentials' list ever since. The porters were already carrying between 14-20 kgs. I was now carrying the lightest pack I have ever carried (about 8kg). It seemed too easy. My guilt was somewhat eased with the knowledge that the porters were well paid (farm wages x 3) plus they would receive a tip the end of the trip. The locals were getting a fair deal.

As we ascended, the landscape changed again. Yesterday we drove through the bamboo forest, and today we walked up the grassy foothills which contained sparsely distributed trees. The trees gradually became smaller as we ascended, and became less in number until there were none. Next, we reached an acclimatization peak named Mogi Hill (3500m) and we were surrounded by scrubland not dissimilar to Scottish or Welsh moorland. After 10km, we reached the remote Lake Ellis (3450m), the impressive scene of our first camp. The white table was standing to attention on arrival, complete with a red checkered table cloth, sitting under a gazebo. A picture book picnic table, seemingly at odds with its rustic surroundings.

It was only 2 p.m., but the sun's strength already began to wither and we stood in a circle around the table chatting. The clouds arrived in the early afternoon and it began to cool down quickly (thus setting the weather pattern for each day). In the early evening we had some hot food at the picnic table. Everything was there, except a camp fire. After we finished eating we stood around the table, under the gazebo, as if we were selling RAC membership at a UK motorway service station.

The porters had a separate camp about 10 meters away, where they sat on rocks around a large fire. They were chatting and laughing. I looked on with some envy, and wondered if we should all be sharing seats around the same fire: I didn't care much for the picnic table and the gazebo.

The temperature went down to zero at midnight. On top of this was a wind chill and after a cold night we woke up at sunrise to find a glistening frost on the tents. Before breakfast, I wandered over to the porter's camp and warmed myself on their fire. It was difficult to drag myself away, as the sun was too weak to work its magic at 6.a.m.

Day 3. Spirits were soon lifted by the African sunrise over Lake Ellis (3450m)

We were the only party on the mountain, *or were we?* Graham had gone for a toilet trek in the middle of the night to find two red eyes peering at him in the darkness. The plot thickened in the morning, when within five minutes of walking from the camp the guide pointed out some leopard droppings. The guide assured us that leopards were very shy, frightened of humans and he had only seen two in the last ten years whilst trekking these mountains: but the guides words did not allay my fears because all around us were thick scrubs around 2-4 foot high, which was perfect hiding ground for a leopard ambush. I was no expert but I've seen enough Tarzan films to create enough fear in my mind. Besides, the leopard was hungry and it had a family to feed. For a couple of kilometres my senses were alerted, and I looked around at my fellow hikers. Who could I outrun? Maybe Nigel and Liz, as Graham and Sally were marathon fell runners.

As we gained ground, Lake Ellis seemed far below us and the scrubs became smaller and sparser. The terrain became increasingly rocky as we reached 4,000 metres. It seemed as if the air was thinner and breathing was a bit more laboured. Despite this nobody complained or spontaneously collapsed due to altitude sickness. We reached a ridge where we sat down for lunch. The mysterious lobelias trees added a much needed African flavor to a very British highland terrain. At 4200m we joined the main Chogoria path. It was a Tolkien-style path, clinging to the cliffs to the right with a steep drop to the left. Before we approached the lofty cliffs surrounding Lake Michaelson, the guide pointed out the wreckage of an old plane crash from 2003 scattered along the top of the ridge, overlooking Lake Michaelson.

We gave ground and zig-zagged down a very steep path to our next camp, immediately below us; Lake Michaelson. The lake and camp was half surrounded by a curtain of steep Eiger style cliffs. The plastic table was already there, as if by magic. Before we could pay our respects to the table, we noticed several rock hyraxes scurrying around the rocks behind the tents. Hyraxes are a plucky, chirpy mammal which looked like a cross between a beaver and an overweight hamster: some were the size of small cats. The hyraxes were chattering away, and quite curious by our arrival onto their patch. It was also dinner time for the hyraxes.

On this expedition, we had not seen any other people, so it felt like the mountain was *ours*. After exchanging pleasantries we retreated to our tents to seek warmth. I noticed that the porters were huddled behind a large rock… but next to the fire. At this point I was prepared to swap the plastic table, in the exposed icy breeze, for the fire and the warm rocks. At 3950 meters this was going to be another long and cold night. I had realized by now that my coat and sleeping bag were not good enough for this expedition. I had skimped on kit and I was now paying the price. I borrowed a down jacket from Graham, but the sleeping bag was not good enough to keep out the freezing temperatures. The camping expedition was completely different to Alpine expeditions where mountain huts are used for sleeping. The main difference was that the huts were warm in the Alps and the tents were cold on these expeditions. For expeditions you need a seriously warm sleeping bag that can stand up to minus 25 degrees or more. I had balked at the costs of these expensive sleeping bags (why need a sleeping bag for -25 when it only gets to -5 on the mountain…?) And now I was paying the price, in the currency of coldness. The upside on these expeditions is that you can take a large quantity of elaborate kit without carrying it yourself. The porters carried it and they got tipped. That was the deal. With this arrangement there was no excuse for skimping on good quality kit.

Day four.

After another spectacular sunrise, we ascended the steep stairs with the morning sun warming our backs. It was difficult to take your eyes off the picture perfect lake that we were leaving behind as we followed the steep path next to the green grassy banks of the river. I kept on turning around to look at the view of the glacial blue lake surrounded by majestic brown cliffs. The MK six reached the top of the gully, and we were overtaken by the porters again with the white table leading the way like a beacon.

When we reached the top of the cliffs we went through a rocky gateway leading to the wide base of Gorges valley. Another view greeted us; the full glory of the semi–circle of Mount Kenya's peaks lining up before our eyes. We were getting close now. The guide pointed out Lenana, Batian and Nellion peaks.

There were many other distinctive rock features on the ridge including several teeth shaped pinnacles and galleon-like ships with port holes. These rock features had understandably captured the imagination of previous mountaineers, including the three Italian POWs. I had never seen anything like this before: it was a rich tapestry of weird and wonderful rock formations.

The base of the bowl was characterised by hundreds of distinctive lobelia trees. Lobelia trees could be described as thin cactuses crowned with several pineapples heads placed on top. These strangely attractive trees stood around like a scattered army of mysterious statues: they were a good distraction from the exertion of walking at higher altitude. I noticed that as we ascended, Graham seemed to be keeping to regular pace (literally one step immediately in front of the other), and monitoring his heart beat. I decided to drop back and match his steady and measured pace. We were both concerned about altitude sickness. Notably, Graham and myself had not exceeded 4,000 metres before and were probably a bit more wary of entering unchartered altitude territory than the rest of the MK six who already had several 5,000 and 6,000 metre peaks under their belts. The spectre of altitude sickness was daunting and an individual's confidence of physically coping with high altitude could only be increased with a successful track record of high peaks.

After four hours of ascending at a slow pace, or "poley-poley" (in Swahili) to reduce the risk of altitude sickness, we finally reached Simba tarn at 4,600 metres, our final camp before the summit. It seemed like a stone's throw away from the summit ridges. The initial warmth gained from the steep slope ascent disappeared and was replaced by a cold chill as we stood around the camp. Once again we experienced changeable weather in the space of one hour: sun-cloud-hail-sun-cloud. After grabbing a hot drink from the white table, we quickly went into the small mess tent which was now available to generate some stories and communal warmth. We exchanged comments about our respective physical condition. After an early dinner, everybody went off to tents at 7 p.m. I lay awake staring at the roof of my tent wishing I had brought a book.

Day Five.

Eddie came round to our tents at 3a.m. for the wake-up call, although I had already been awake for a few hours, anxious to get moving and generate warmth. We struggled to eat breakfast, but managed to set off at 4.15 a.m. It was almost completely dark, except for the moonlight. For the entire expedition we had enjoyed the priceless privilege of having the mountain to ourselves… until we heard some loud American voices. As we were putting on our rucksacks they cut through the middle of our camp, and we followed immediately, our MK six quietly focusing on our steps going forward, heads bowed with head torches lighting up our plodding footsteps. Call me old fashioned but it seemed rude to break the silence in the darkness. The pace quickened as our guide appeared intent on overtaking the American group. Graham questioned what had happened to the Poley-Poley policy (this had been thrown out with the kitchen sink). The party in front were getting tired and one or two stragglers were stopping occasionally, holding up both parties which had now merged together in one long train hoping to reach the summit in time for sunrise. We heard some German and Korean accents, and now the mountain had an international feel to it, giving MK a bit more kudos.

It was difficult progress on the steep path, powdered with a thin layer of dust and small pebbles, combined with light-headedness requiring extra focus and careful balance as a slip would cause a dangerous domino effect on those behind. We were close now.

As the path looped around the final approach to the Lenana summit, behind us we could see that in distance there was a huge, carpeted bank of clouds. Sitting above the clouds on the horizon was a thin orange glowing line, a sight I cannot recall seeing before. This was the impressive prequel to the sunrise.

We were then surprised to find some cable wire fixed to the rock and a small section of ladders leading the summit. This additional fixed climbing equipment seemed almost as unnecessary as the white plastic table. All became clear when saw a sign next to the ladders "The highest via feratta in the world".

I reached the summit, feeling slightly giddy and relieved. Lenana's rounded peak gave us the spectacular views of sunrise in the east, Kilimanjaro in the south sitting somewhere below the clouds in the distance.

To the immediate west was the impressive Batian Peak (5,199 metre) with its steep walls. Understandably, unclimbable for many, including great mountaineers such as Ellis, and the determined Italian POWs. Mackinder deserved his recognition of conquering Batian Peak in 1929.

Back to 2016. After 15 minutes of frantic handshakes, hugs, photographs, and congratulations, we left the summit as the cold started to kick-in once more.

 We hurried down the scree slopes, sliding in paces but trying to avoid tripping over. Now glowing in the pride and satisfaction of having reached the summit, the pressure was off, and any altitude concerns had evaporated away. We quickly passed those hikers who were slowly and painfully ascending the final reaches.

We arrived back at the high camp Simba tarn (4,600 metre) for a quick breakfast, which almost seemed like an unnecessary interruption to the adrenalin fueled descent. However it was only around 8 a.m. and we had a long day of walking ahead, so we clumsily skidded and slipped down another steep scree slope into the Mackinder valley (the Sirimon route), past the well-established Shipton Hut and Shipton's cave. More sightings of rock hyraxes, tropical birds, and leopard droppings on foot. Above us, the impressively high sided and pinnacled ridges of the Mackinder valley. As we clocked up the miles the views eventually deteriorated along with the weather, as we soon became surrounded by cooler low clouds and rather bland moorland. Although it was unfair to compare the lower reaches of the valley path with the summit areas, this well-trodden exit path was definitely the quick and dirty route to Mount Kenya.

We finally reached the old Moses camp after clocking up a decent hiking shift of 20 km. It was a straightforward camp. With the expedition almost complete now all we had to do was to get a good night's sleep ahead of the final day. This task evaded me as my hot water bottle somehow leaked in my sleeping bag, so I threw the wet bag outside the tent in the middle of the night, used some makeshift blankets and clothes to try and keep warm for the duration, dreaming (whilst awake) of my next purchase an expensive and warm sleeping bag.

Day Six

The next morning I found my discarded sleeping bag frozen solid, covered in white frost to the amusement of the MK six, and especially Geoff. At the lowest and final camp Moses, we were still at a height of 3,300 metre.

We set off from the camp at a fast pace, downhill, actually crossing the equator and being surprised to see that nobody had painted a line across the earth. The assistant cook/guide said that our expedition was the 'last of the season'. He told me that the number of hikers attempting Mount Kenya was very small, especially compared to Kilimanjaro. He went on to say that the marketing should be done by "white people" (meaning Europeans) and not "black people" (meaning locals). The logic here was that the clientele are mainly Europeans. The reality of expedition closure began to sink in when the tips were distributed at the "tipping ceremony" and the old gear we donated to the Porters was spread out on the car park for the sixteen porters to undertake the serious business of selecting three items per man – for keeps. Geoff gave an appropriately British thank you speech to the expedition party. I was really pleased to see one of the porters wearing my green jungle hat (it suited him) but I never saw who got my old boots (they were old enough to walk away on their own).The MK six shook hands with all of the local porters (who had kept their distance all through the trip, and even now, avoided all eye contact with us). We boarded the old faithful land cruiser with a degree of sadness as the adventure was now over. Heading towards Nairobi, we were getting slowly closer to a shower, and some well-earned cold beers.

■■■

EPILOGUE

Photographs alone cannot capture the beauty of the mountains or the sense of adventure experienced by those who choose to venture there. These journals are based on contemporary journals of selected walks – an attempt to record some of my hillwalking experiences. There is a blur between fact and fiction and have tried to remain faithful to the former. Notwithstanding this, experience has taught me that everybody has their own perspective of unacceptable risk and people try to strike a balance between adventure and safety exposure. In many circumstances there is no firm set of rules. Everybody has their own comfort zone that they are trying to escape from… if it's "safe" to do so. Most hillwalkers simply enjoy the walks to reconnect with nature and to find a peace of mind in the great outdoors; for others it's the challenge and the exhilaration of standing on top of a hill or a mountain; it doesn't really matter because it's just great to get away from your laptop and get out there. The irony is that I am sitting in doors; hours on end, typing these words on my laptop has not escaped me.

I would like to thank my walking companions through the years; some who did not feature in this journal due to the two main reasons: firstly I only started writing the journal in 2007; secondly, I selected sixteen walks for this book, which is only a small sample from the hundreds of walks that my friends and I completed. In alphabetical order; Andy, Aran, Chris, Geoff, Gordon, Howard and Ric at various stages between 1993 and 2016 have been truly great walking companions and friends – thanks for the great memories, and hopefully we can do some more whilst our legs are still working.

I must thank my good friend (and author) Ric Coady, who for reasons unknown, foolishly agreed to do some adept editing work on this book. The remaining errors (and there will be) are entirely my own.

It was never an objective to create a "walker's guide". I don't have the knowledge or the beard to qualify for this honour. In this journal I have explained my brief flirtation with mountaineering and the dark arts of rope knots and all that bloody equipment, is quite a challenge to a middle aged man. In hindsight it was a mistake when I stopped going to the local Cubs group in the 1970s - because it clashed with *The Six Million Dollar Man* which was on ITV, every Thursday, at 7.30 p.m. To be fair I was only eight years old back then…. and Lee Majors was a really impressive runner.

On a final note whilst you are heading to the mountains (inspired by this book of course) kitted out in your essential designer label walking gear – never forget the old saying: *"There are old mountaineers, and bold mountaineers – but never both"*.

****

Printed in Great Britain
by Amazon

76316427R00098